If It *Doesn't* Fit

If It *Doesn't* Fit

LESSONS FROM A LIFE IN THE LAW

Gerald F. Uelmen

To order additional copies of this book, contact:
Xlibris
1-888-795-4274
www.Xlibris.com
Orders@Xlibris.com
734016

CONTENTS

INTRODUCTION

A REFLECTION IS a look back; a rumination is a chewing over, like a cow chews its cud. This book contains both. Most of the reflections were written about events and issues in which I participated as I experienced them. The ruminations are current thoughts about the same events and issues after chewing them over. They contain some pride, some regrets, and, hopefully, some insights.

As I approach the fiftieth anniversary of my admission to the bar, I count myself lucky in the variety of lawyer roles in which I have been cast. While still in law school, I had the opportunity to "try on" some potential legal careers to see if they "fit." A summer clerkship with a busy Washington law firm convinced me that fighting over other people's money was not where I wanted to spend my life. Another summer clerkship in the bowels of the Department of Interior convinced me that I did not want to be a government "office lawyer." I wanted to be in the courtrooms, where I believed the real action was. After graduating from Georgetown Law Center in 1965, I began my career representing indigent defendants in the courts of Washington, DC, as a Prettyman Fellow, the first experiment to have law graduates serve a supervised "internship." It was an exciting year that honed my courtroom skills and fully confirmed my goal to become a trial lawyer. I then moved "back home" to Los Angeles and accepted a position as a federal prosecutor, specializing in organized crime investigations and prosecutions. I found that I could fit on either side of the criminal courtroom with equal comfort. After four years, I moved to the world of academia, becoming a law school professor. I loved the classroom interaction with students as well as the scholarly research but wanted to keep one foot in the courtroom. I was able to balance a full-time teaching career with law practice, confining my courtroom ventures to briefing and arguing appeals, with an occasional foray into trial courts in a consulting role, assisting other lawyers litigating motions and evidentiary issues.

The life of a law professor also fit well with the family life to which I aspired. I grew up in a family of eight children, five of whom predeceased my parents. Strong family ties have been a constant in my life through triumphs and tragedies. With my wife, Martha, who herself pursued successive careers as a nursing professor and a family law practitioner and mediator, we raised three children. Our two daughters both took vows and still dedicate their life to the pursuit of unity as members of the Focolare, a Catholic movement that has strongly influenced the course of our lives. Our son became a successful composer of music for video games, married a brilliant lawyer, and gifted us with two grandsons, the current delight of our lives.

I became active in leadership of the California criminal defense bar and ventured into the political arena to oppose ballot initiatives that sought to dismantle constitutional protections of the accused under the misleading banner of victims' rights, to oppose the death penalty, and to support the independence of elected justices of the California Supreme Court. I also collaborated with a couple lawyers who shared my sense of humor, producing two volumes that demonstrated that legal humor is not an oxymoron. Both are still in print. In 1986, I relocated from Los Angeles to the San Francisco Bay Area to accept a position as dean of Santa Clara University School of Law. My goals to enhance the diversity of the faculty and student body, engage the law school in social justice issues, increase the visibility of Santa Clara law in the community, and introduce more real-life experience into the law school curriculum were largely met.

After eight fruitful years as a law school dean, I was preparing to return to the classroom when I received the invitation to join the "Dream Team" representing O. J. Simpson in his Los Angeles murder trial. It turned out to be two of the most challenging years in my professional life. In spare moments during the trial, I also achieved a lifetime ambition of becoming a playwright, authoring a one-actor play on the life of William Jennings Bryan, which was subsequently produced in Omaha, Chicago, and Santa Clara. After the O. J. verdict, I returned to the classroom with lots of "war stories" for my students and enough fodder for two books about the tactics used during the trial. Twenty years later, I realize the blank stares my students give me when I start talking about the O. J. trial are because they were in kindergarten in 1994.

I also returned to the courtrooms to advance the right of seriously ill persons to have access to medicinal marijuana and had the treasured experience of briefing and arguing (and losing) a case on their behalf in the U.S. Supreme Court. My scholarly interests turned to the work of the California Supreme Court; and in partnership with an accomplished historian, I researched and coauthored a biography of the court's longest-serving justice, Stanley Mosk. In 2004, I was tapped to serve as executive director of the California Commission on the Fair Administration of Justice, coordinating a four-year inquiry into the causes of wrongful convictions and the dysfunction of California's death penalty. When the continuation of California's death penalty law was placed on the ballot in 2012, I eagerly joined the political battle to eliminate it, ending in a narrow loss.

In each of these roles, I wrote about my endeavors, filling law reviews, legal journals, and newspaper op-ed pages with what I hoped were thoughtful, historical, and sometimes humorous observations and justifications. Today, from the vantage point of imminent retirement, I reread what I wrote and ruminate on the value of it all. Did I spend my life in pursuit of unachievable goals, tilting at windmills like Don Quixote? Could I have better served myself and my family by reaping the financial rewards available to a lawyer with my talents? Was my pursuit of "justice" really a chase after rainbows? I strongly suspect that the answer to all three of these questions is yes, but I would still do it all over again.

Many of the questions with which I have struggled during my legal career still trouble lawyers and judges, as well as the students I have taught, in their continuing search for justice. The system of justice in which I operated will creak on, providing ways for some to narrow the gulf that separates haves from have-nots and providing for others the opportunity to widen that gulf. It is my sincere hope that the reflections and ruminations I have collected in this volume will offer deeper understanding of the events and causes that occupied my life as well as occasional insights for those who continue in their own search for justice.

I

The O. J. Trial

1

"If it doesn't fit, you must acquit."

THE FIFTEEN MINUTES of fame that Andy Warhol promised everyone came my way in 1994–1995 when I served on the "Dream Team" representing O. J. Simpson in his Los Angeles murder trial. I really had no idea what I was stepping into when I accepted Robert Shapiro's invitation to come to LA and assist him in representing the famous football star. I had never met O. J. and was only vaguely familiar with his exploits on and off the field. I was never a rabid football fan or a fan of any sport. My current love of baseball came late in life.

The timing with which this opportunity arose was quite propitious. I was "retiring" from service as dean of Santa Clara University School of Law and looking forward to go on a full year of sabbatical leave, to write a play, and to teach a semester of criminal procedure at Stanford Law School as a visiting professor. I was packing up my boxes when I received a phone call from my friend Robert Shapiro in Los Angeles. Bob and I had previously collaborated in the defense of Christian Brando in a Los Angeles homicide trial and worked smoothly together to achieve an excellent result. Bob was coordinating the team of lawyers and experts that would serve O. J. Simpson in his upcoming murder trial. Three days later, I was on a plane to Los Angeles. My "sabbatical projects" suddenly included direct participation in the "trial of the century." My parents still had a spare room where I could roost during the frequent forays to LA, which filled the next two years. My role was primarily to guide the defense team through the intricacies of the California Evidence Code, with which I had become intimately familiar both in teaching and writing for the practicing bar. I prepared and argued motions to dismiss the grand jury, served as co-counsel for the preliminary hearing, then litigated all the pretrial motions to suppress or exclude evidence from the trial. I never appeared before the jury during the lengthy trial that ensued. My appearances were focused on the legal issues that occasionally interrupted the trial, such as the admissibility of tape recordings of the racist rants of Detective Mark Fuhrman, and the preparation and argument surrounding the instructions of law to be presented at the trial's conclusion. But every aspect of the trial was a collaborative endeavor, and Johnnie Cochran asked all of us for suggestions as he prepared for the closing arguments. My response to that request was the following memorandum, which became the source of the most memorable line in Cochran's stunning summation:

TO: JOHNNIE COCHRAN, JR.
FROM: JERRY UELMEN
RE: THOUGHTS AND SUGGESTIONS FOR CLOSING ARGUMENT
JUNE 28, 1995

The gloves not fitting was not just a home run from an evidentiary standpoint. I think it provides a theme that you can use to write a symphony for your closing argument. The theme even rhymes: If it doesn't fit, you must acquit. That theme will appear in the jury instructions. The one instruction we can count on, because both sides are requesting it, which will be the most significant instruction the jury hears from our perspective, is CALJIC 2.01. I think you should make this instruction the center-piece of your summation.

"... a finding of guilt as to any crime may not be based on circumstantial evidence unless the proved circumstances are not only (1) consistent with the theory that the defendant is guilty of the crime, but (2) cannot be reconciled with any other rational conclusion. Further, each fact which is essential to complete a set of circumstances necessary to establish the defendant's guilt must be proved beyond a reasonable doubt. In other words, before an inference essential to establish guilt may be found to have been proved beyond a reasonable doubt, each fact or circumstance upon which such inference necessarily rests must be proven beyond a reasonable doubt. Also, if the circumstantial evidence is susceptible of two reasonable interpretations, one of which points to the defendant's guilt and the other to his innocence, you must adopt that interpretation which points to the defendant's innocence, and reject that interpretation that points to his guilt. If, on the other hand, one interpretation of such evidence appears to you to be reasonable and the other interpretation to be unreasonable, you must accept the reasonable interpretation and reject the unreasonable."

I would suggest getting this instruction on a large placard so it can be displayed during your argument. The meaning of the instruction can truly be paraphrased to say, "If it doesn't fit, you must acquit." The evidence must fit the interpretation of the facts that leads to a conclusion of guilt. If it doesn't fit, then the conclusion must be rejected. The problem with the prosecution's case is that there are lots of places where the evidence doesn't fit the picture they want the jury to see. What they suggest is if the evidence doesn't fit the picture, then ignore it, or discard it or suppress it or restructure it. We can present dozens of examples of that. But what the instructions to the jury require if the evidence doesn't fit the picture is that the jury must acquit. The evidence must be consistent with the theory that the defendant is guilty, and not reconcilable with any other rational conclusion.

The jury will be offered two conflicting scenarios or theories of what the evidence shows. They can be summarized in story form, which is the way the jury will conceptualize them. The prosecution "story" essentially goes:

JEALOUS MAN STALKS EX-WIFE;
STABS HER AND MALE VISITOR IN MURDEROUS RAGE;
LEAVES TRAIL OF BLOOD TO HIS HOME;
BARELY CATCHES PLANE TO CHICAGO;
IN HIS RUSH, LEAVES ONE GLOVE AT MURDER SCENE,
AND ONE GLOVE BEHIND HIS HOUSE.

The competing defense theory or "story" has been presented without O.J. even having to testify:

MAN IS AT HOME PREPARING FOR A BUSINESS TRIP;
HE HAS HAD A FULL DAY: EARLY GOLF GAME,
CHILDREN'S PROGRAM;
HE DOZES OFF, THEN TAKES A QUICK SHOWER;
HE BARELY CATCHES HIS PLANE TO CHICAGO;
SOMEONE ELSE MURDERS HIS WIFE AND MALE VISITOR
FOR REASONS UNKNOWN;
SOMEONE ELSE SEEKS TO IMPLICATE HIM AS THE MOST
OBVIOUS SUSPECT;
THE INVESTIGATION BECOMES A TRAGIC
COMBINATION OF SLOPPY ERRORS AND COVER-UPS TO
ACHIEVE HIS CONVICTION.

The jury's job is not to decide which of these two scenarios is more reasonable. They must find the first scenario is reasonable and the second is unreasonable. If they find they are both reasonable scenarios, they must adopt the second one, which points to innocence, and reject the first one, which points to guilt. To convict, they must find every fact essential to reach the conclusion of guilt has been proven beyond a reasonable doubt. Thus, even if they think the second scenario is not reasonable, they must still acquit if they find that any of the facts necessary to prove the first scenario don't fit the evidence beyond a reasonable doubt. If it doesn't fit, you must acquit. More appropriately, if you have a reasonable doubt whether it fits or not, you must acquit!

The lack of a fit between the evidence and the prosecution scenario can then be played out again and again as you review the evidence:

1. JEALOUS MAN STALKS EX-WIFE.

The attempt to portray O.J. as a morose, angry jealous man simply doesn't fit the evidence. The videotape of him saying good-by to the Brown family after the concert should be replayed. The photo of him presenting the flowers he had rushed out to buy to give to his daughter should be again displayed. Does this evidence fit the picture the prosecution is trying to present? Is this the picture of a jealous man seething with rage?

The evidence presented of prior arguments and fights between O.J. and Nicole also don't fit the scenario. Remind the jury that

GERALD F. UELMEN

the only reason this evidence was presented was to show identity and motive. The only inference the prosecution can urge is that the prior arguments are so similar to the murder that the same jealous husband is responsible for both. The prior incidents, however, don't fit the brutal execution by stealth that occurred June 12, 1994. The prior arguments had lots of common elements: they were loud, angry confrontations, with lots of screaming, hollering and throwing things around—broken pictures, etc. In most cases, they were preceded by the consumption of alcohol by both O.J. and Nicole. New Year's Eve, or partying with friends. Nothing of the sort occurred on June 12, so the inference that one led to the other is so weak it should be disregarded. It certainly can't be concluded that it was proven beyond a reasonable doubt. It doesn't fit, and if it doesn't fit, you must acquit.

2. O.J. STABBED AND SLIT THE THROATS OF THE VICTIMS IN A MURDEROUS RAGE.

Again, the evidence doesn't fit the picture of O.J. Simpson that emerges from the evidence. It doesn't fit the testimony of Kato Kaelin, describing going out to get a hamburger. Where was O.J.'s mind the last time Kato saw him? It was on the trip to Chicago, thinking about whether he had the right change to tip the limo driver and the porters at the airport. It doesn't fit the testimony of the limo driver, whose description of O.J. is more consistent with a man in a rush to pack up and catch a plane than it is of a man who just slit the throats of two persons after a ferocious struggle. It doesn't fit the physical evidence of the condition of O.J.'s body after his arrest. Not a scratch or a bruise, other than the tiny cut on one finger.

Even the cut on the finger doesn't match the explanation the prosecution wants the jury to infer. There are no corresponding cuts on the glove, and there is blood and broken glass in the hotel room in Chicago. [Incidentally, I'm not sure the broken glass and bloody towel from Chicago are in evidence. If not, we should put them in. It offers us an opportunity to explain the cut without O.J. having to testify, and there is no evidence at all of his explanation of having cut himself before he left Chicago. In fact, we may put the prosecution in the awkward position of having to offer his statement in rebuttal, to rebut the inference that the Chicago cut explains the injury to his finger!]. The murderous rage doesn't fit the evidence of his demeanor at the airport or on the airplane. Could someone who just slit the throats of two people after a furious struggle present the jovial and relaxed demeanor that O.J. presents one hour later?

The murderous rage doesn't fit the evidence suggesting that there may have been more than one assailant, including the coroner's suggestion that more than one knife may have been responsible for the wounds. The prosecution was so obsessed with suppressing this evidence they didn't even call the coroner who did the autopsies to testify. But you can't simply ignore or discard evidence because it doesn't fit the scenario that leads to guilt. If it doesn't fit, you must acquit.

3.   THE TRAIL OF BLOOD.

The prosecution scenario is that O.J. left a trail of blood from the crime scene to his bedroom. The evidence of where blood was found does not fit this scenario. The drops on the driveway lead to or from the front door, not to where the glove was found. There was no blood found on the white carpet leading up the steps to his bedroom. If he had blood on his socks, why didn't it leave stains on the carpet? There was no bloody clothing found, with the exception of the socks. Yet no blood on the socks was found until a month after they were seized.

The pattern of the blood stains suggests they were not all left at the same time. How do we account for the dramatic differences in the quantity of DNA recovered from different stains? The evidence doesn't fit the testimony of the tow truck driver who transported the vehicle from the print shack to Vertel's. He didn't see any blood stains in the Bronco, and entered the Bronco himself. The number 4 allele on the steering wheel doesn't fit either, suggesting a strong probability of a donor other than O.J. or the victims.

The blood trail thus leads in two different directions. In one direction, it leads to O.J.'s guilt. In the other direction, it leads to his innocence. If the prosecution has not proven every fact on the trail that leads to guilt beyond a reasonable doubt, you must acquit. And even if they have, if the trail that leads to innocence is just as reasonable, you must accept the trail to innocence. If it doesn't fit, you must acquit.

4.   O.J. BARELY CATCHES HIS PLANE FOR CHICAGO.

The prosecution scenario is that the dark figure that the limo driver saw entering the house was O.J. returning from the murder.

The defense scenario is that it was O.J. alright, but he was just getting luggage out for the trip. The fact that the luggage was already out and waiting when the driver pulled in doesn't fit the prosecution scenario. The short lapse of time between O.J.'s entry to the house and his appearance for departure didn't provide adequate time to get cleaned up and dispose of a murder weapon, bloody clothing, etc. The location of the glove behind the house is also inconsistent with the prosecution scenario. The circumstances of the limo pickup don't fit the prosecution scenario. In fact, they are more consistent with the defense scenario that points to innocence. If it doesn't fit, you must acquit.

5. IN HIS RUSH, HE LEAVES ONE GLOVE AT THE MURDER SCENE, ONE BEHIND THE HOUSE.
   The testimony of Detective Mark Fuhrman does not fit this scenario. The position of the glove, its relationship to other evidence, are not consistent with O.J. having dropped it. The glove may have been used by the murderer, but it is just as reasonable to believe it was found at the murder scene.
   Most important, the gloves do not fit O.J. They are in the same condition they were when they were recovered, and shrinkage cannot be attributed to blood stains. They are too small, and no amount of prosecution manipulating or explaining or experimenting can make them bigger. The evidence doesn't fit the scenario that leads to guilt. If it doesn't fit, you must acquit.

A similar review should then be undertaken of the defense scenario, showing that all the evidence is consistent with that scenario. But it must be emphasized that the defense doesn't have to prove any scenario, or offer any explanation for the evidence. The burden is on the prosecution to prove every fact essential to lead to a conclusion of guilt beyond a reasonable doubt. If the evidence is inconsistent with such a conclusion, the jury must reject the conclusion and acquit.
   IF IT DOESN'T FIT, YOU MUST ACQUIT.

Later in the trial, after I had prepared our proposed jury instructions and argued them to Judge Ito, I prepared a follow-up memo with more suggestions for the closing arguments:

TO: JOHNNIE COCHRAN, JR. AND BARRY SCHECK
FROM: JERRY UELMEN
RE: FINAL THOUGHTS ON FINAL ARGUMENTS
DATE: SEPT. 24, 1995

1. As I reread the alternative scenarios I laid out in the memo
    of June 28, I realized the opening Kelberg gave us needs to
    be incorporated onto the alternative scenario that points to
    innocence, as follows:

He dozes off then takes a quick shower; he runs out to retrieve
something from his Bronco, and cuts himself on the finger. The
tiny cut drips a few small drops of blood, but is so small it isn't even
noticed by anyone else. He barely catches his plane to Chicago.

2. I was delighted to hear you will do some bible thumping, Johnnie.
    Attached is a piece I did for the L.A. Times two years ago on
    the appropriateness of biblical quotations in jury arguments.
    This morning's Gospel reading reminded me that the wonderful
    jury instruction about rejecting all of the testimony of a liar is
    endorsed by Jesus in Chapter 16 of Luke, verse 10: "He who is
    honest (faithful) in a small thing is honest also in much; and he
    who is dishonest in a very little thing is also dishonest in much."

3. When you argue lack of motive from the evidence about calls
    to Paula Barbieri and other indications that O. J. was putting
    together a new life without Nicole, be sure to quote the jury
    instruction on motive. Although motive is not an element of the
    crime, "absence of motive may tend to establish innocence." Just
    the evidence on lack of motive is enough to raise a reasonable
    doubt.

4. All of the evidence about other incidents between O. J. and
    Nicole were admitted on the theory that inferences could be
    drawn from their similarity to the murders. One question
    you may want to leave for Marcia if she hammers us with this
    evidence, is to ask where are the similarities? The prior incidents
    were loud arguments. No incident after 1989, when O. J. agreed
    that that their prenuptial agreement would be void if he ever

GERALD F. UELMEN

laid a hand on Nicole, ever involved any assault or even a threat of physical harm. The prior incidents never involved stealth. O. J.'s arrival was so loud and noisy everyone in the neighborhood would have been aware of it.

5. When they argue our failure to call witnesses referred to in our opening statement, as they surely will, I like Johnnie's idea of listing all the witnesses we called who were not promised in our opening. But it's also worth reminding the jurors that opening statements were given nine months ago, and they were an attempt to anticipate what evidence the prosecution promised to put on. Their failure to deliver on their promises obviated the need to call many of our witnesses. For example, since they never called Keith Zlomsowitch, we never needed the testimony of Dr. Lenore Walker. We also need to emphasize that these arguments are really an attempt to shift the burden of proof. You may want to quote jury instruction 2.11 which the court gave:

> "Neither side is required to call as witnesses all persons who may have been present at any of the events disclosed by the evidence or who may appear to have some knowledge of these events, or to produce all objects or documents mentioned or suggested by the evidence."

While this also suggests the prosecution doesn't have to call all the available witnesses, their failure to prove every element of their case beyond a reasonable doubt requires an acquittal.

6. I'm putting together a memo to be filed that anticipates the improper arguments we anticipate may be made by the prosecution, but I wanted to remind Barry of the privilege objection if they argue any failure to call experts for any purpose. While I'm afraid we waived this objection for experts we mentioned in our opening statement, like Cary Mullis and Leonore Walker, the objection is still a valid one for any other experts. See People v. Bittaker, 48 Cal.3d 1046, 1104, 259 Cal. Rptr. 630 (1989):

"The prosecution may not comment upon a defendant's failure to call a witness if the defendant has a privilege to bar disclosure of that witness's testimony. Evid. Code Section 913."

7. *PASSION!!!!*

The following op-ed article, which I published in the *Los Angeles Times* on November 19, 1991, was attached to the September 24 memo:

The Nincompoops Aren't in the Jury Box.

Karl S. Chambers of York, Pa. was convicted of beating an elderly woman to death with an ax handle because she refused to turn over her wallet. The final words of the deputy district attorney to the jury deciding his fate were, "Karl Chambers has taken a life. As the Bible says, 'and the murderer shall be put to death.'" Defense counsel objected. The trial judge sustained the objection and told the jury to ignore the biblical exhortation.

This month, in a 6–1 ruling, the Pennsylvania Supreme Court reversed Chambers' death sentence on the sole ground that the prosecutor quoted the Bible in his closing argument. In what is easily the dumbest decision of the year, the court said the judge's instruction to the jury wasn't enough, and that a mistrial should have been declared.

The Justices sent a powerful message to prosecutors. "We now admonish all prosecutors that reliance in any manner upon the Bible or any other religious writing in support of the imposition of a penalty of death is reversible error *per se* and may subject violators to disciplinary action."

That's the wrong message. The best cure for Bible-thumping prosecutors is Bible-thumping defense lawyers. If Karl Chambers were being defended by Clarence Darrow, there wouldn't have even been an objection to the prosecutor's argument. Darrow would simply have pulled a Bible out of his beat-up briefcase and turned to Exodus. He would have reminded the jurors that the same Bible that commands the execution of murderers also commands the execution of adulterers, witches, those who have sex with animals, and anyone who reviles or curses his mother or father.

He would have noted the Bible contains some curious exceptions, such as the one for a man who beats his slave to death. "If the slave does not die for a couple of days, then the man shall not be punished—for the slave is his property." Finally, Darrow would have turned to the New Testament, and read to the jurors the words of Jesus Christ when he was invited to participate in an execution. "Let anyone among you who is without sin be the first to cast a stone at her."

The point is not whether the Bible supports or condemns capital punishment. The point is that jurors are intelligent enough to give the Bible the weight it deserves, and lawyers should be free to address jurors as though they are intelligent human beings. As former Court of Appeal Justice Robert Gardner put it, "A juror is not some kind of dithering nincompoop, brought in from never-never-land and exposed to the harsh realities of life for the first time in the jury box."

All too often, the dithering nincompoops in today's courtrooms are the lawyers and the judges. One cannot read the great jury arguments by lawyers of the past and not be impressed by all the literary and biblical allusions at their command. They were widely read, and they rightfully assumed that the jurors they addressed were too. Consider Darrow's denunciation of informer Harry Orchard in the trial of Bill Haywood for the murder of Idaho Gov. Frank Steunenberg:

> "Why, gentlemen, if Harry Orchard were George Washington, and if he was impeached and contradicted by as many as Harry Orchard has been, George Washington would go out of it disgraced and counted the Ananias of the age."

If Darrow were a Pennsylvania prosecutor, that argument would be reversible *per se*. The reference to Ananias comes from Chapter 5 of the Acts of the Apostles, where Ananias was struck dead for lying to the apostle Peter. The allusion would not be lost on modern jurors. They still read the Bible occasionally. It's the lawyers who don't.

The dumbing down of America has lots of helpers. They now include six Justices of the Supreme Court of Pennsylvania. It's doubtful that their decision will save any murderers from execution. It may not even help Karl Chambers, who faces a new penalty trial with no Bibles allowed. But their decision will certainly render courtrooms more sterile, colorless and divorced from the real flesh and blood of ordinary people. Just like the classrooms, legislatures and governor's mansions.

Note: At Karl Chambers's retrial, he was again sentenced to death, a sentence that was upheld on a second appeal to the Pennsylvania Supreme Court. In 2002, however, that court granted habeas corpus relief on the ground that the jury had not been properly instructed on mitigating circumstances.

Johnnie Cochran's closing argument was a spellbinder, and the most memorable line turned out to be the refrain: "If it doesn't fit, you must acquit." If you google the line, you get 118,000 hits. Less than three thousand attribute the line to me. My favorite attribution is the entry in *The Oxford Dictionary of American Quotations*:

> The rhyme, often misquoted as "If the glove doesn't fit you must acquit," was suggested to Mr. Cochran by a member of his legal team, Gerald Uelmen, but was so strongly identified with him that, as he wrote in his 1996 memoir, *Journey to Justice,* he believed it was "the line by which I will be remembered." And judging from his obituary in the New York Times (March 30, 2005) he was right.

Johnnie, of course, should be remembered for much more than that. My own tribute to the memory of Johnnie Cochran, published in the *California Criminal Defense Practice Reporter*, reads as follows:

Lessons From Johnnie Cochran

How often I've wished I had videotapes available to illustrate the great courtroom arguments by giants like Clarence Darrow. All we have are written transcripts, and even the best dramatizations don't show us the sources of his persuasive power. But Johnnie Cochran has left lawyers with a very rich legacy: his finest moments in the courtroom are all available on videotape.

The key to Cochran's phenomenal success was his ability to connect with jurors. I was absolutely amazed at what he could achieve with twenty minutes of *voir dire* questioning while selecting the O.J. jury. When the jury selection was finished, he said, "Those jurors are my people, all of them, not just the black folks. I know their hearts, and they know mine. And when the time comes, that's how I'm going to speak to them: heart to heart." The "heart to heart" of his closing argument in the O.J. case will always stand as a classic example of courtroom persuasion, but the moment I most remember was the pretrial argument over whether jurors would be allowed to hear that Detective Mark Furhman used the "N-word." "African Americans live with offensive words, offensive looks, offensive treatment every day of their lives," he thundered, "but yet they still believe in this country. And to say that our jurors, because they hear this offensive word, to say they can't be fair is absolutely outrageous." How lucky we are that future students can see the passion as they hear the words!

After the trial, I collaborated with Johnnie in producing a video of excerpts from his closing argument, which we called "Recipe for a Great Closing Argument." There were eight points to Johnnie's recipe for a great summation:

(1) *Tell a story*. His narratives were colorful and laced with humor. Remember the knit cap?
(2) *Be a weaver*. He used the line, "If it doesn't fit, you must acquit" as a theme to weave together all the strands of his arguments.
(3) *Pound the Bible*. While the appellate courts now frown on biblical allusions, Johnny made clever use of the Book of Luke, which suggests if you can't trust your servant in small matters, you cannot trust him in large matters.
(4) *Be a believer*. Johnnie never apologized for his passion and zeal. He looked jurors in the eyes and said, "It's about what's right."
(5) *Pounce on failures*. He made prosecutors squirm as he described their many mistakes.
(6) *Point the finger*. Some were turned off by his comparison of Detective Fuhrman to Hitler, but it was made in the context of Fuhrman's genocidal fantasies, like lining black politicians up against a wall and shooting them. Detectives Van Atter and Lange became the "twin devils of deception."
(7) *Ask some questions*. Johnnie asked fifteen, and none of them were answered in the prosecution's rebuttal.

(8) *End with a zinger.* Johnnie's was "Someone has taken these children's mother. I hope your decision won't take their father."

I am confident many young lawyers will look to Johnnie Cochran as a model of the kind of lawyer they want to be, just as so many lawyers of my generation looked to Clarence Darrow, and just as Johnnie himself looked to Thurgood Marshall. As lawyers today, we need heroes more than ever. There should be a "Lawyer's Hall of Fame," like the Baseball Hall of Fame in Cooperstown, New York, where the achievements of great American lawyers can be enshrined. We belong to a profession that should be proud of its heroes, and we should look to their lives to provide inspiration for our own. And we should look to their videotapes when we need ideas for a powerful closing argument!

2

The Five Hardest Lessons*

P ERHAPS THE O. J. trial is best understood as a cultural phenomenon rather than a lesson plan. Any event that captures such widespread public attention for such a sustained period will have profound cultural repercussions. The slow white Bronco was transformed from a vehicle to a metaphor. A whole new galaxy of celebrities was introduced: Kato Kaelin, Mark Fuhrman, Lance Ito, Marcia Clark, and Johnnie Cochran. The N-word will never be thought of in the same way after the racist rants of Detective Fuhrman.

As a law professor who spent his sabbatical right in the middle of it all, however, I kept looking for lessons. I'd like to share the five hardest lessons I took away from my own experience. I say they're the "hardest" lessons not because they are difficult to comprehend. Most of them are obvious. But they're "hard" because there are no simple solutions to remedy them. Yet for each of them, we've seen simplistic remedies proposed by those who were unhappy with the verdict, with little thought being given to long-term consequences. As H. L. Mencken once said, for every problem, there's an obvious solution that is quick, easy . . . and wrong.

Let me start with lesson number 1: *we all wear tinted lenses, but we don't all wear blinders.* This lesson was brought home to me as I tuned in to the pundits and commentators after a day in court. They described the day's events like a football game, but what I found most amazing is that the same event would be described as a touchdown or a twenty-yard loss. It didn't take me long to figure out in advance what spin would be put on a day's events by which commentators because they all saw the events through lenses that were tinted. Once they came to a conclusion as to the appropriate outcome, they tended to attach greater weight to the evidence that supported that outcome and lesser weight to the evidence that would undercut it. It worked both ways, with pro-prosecution as well as pro-defense pundits. It's a very normal human response.

In the courtroom, we can deal with this tendency head-on by making jurors take an oath that they will keep an open mind until they have heard all the evidence and constantly reminding them of their obligation to do so. Judge Ito delivered these admonitions on a daily basis. Frankly, it did not surprise me at all that the verdict of public opinion was different from the verdict of our jury. The public didn't take the oath that the jurors took and didn't have to follow the admonitions.

I don't mean to suggest that jurors don't wear tinted lenses too. Obviously, like the rest of us, their life experiences will affect the credibility they give to particular witnesses or the weight they give to some evidence. That's why it's so important that juries represent the diversity of life experiences in a community. In the O. J. case, however, the jurors wore something else besides the tinted lenses we all wear. They wore blinders.

Because the jurors were sequestered, they didn't see the press conferences arranged by the lawyers and the families of the victims. They didn't hear the spin of the commentators. They only saw and heard the evidence in the courtroom. Thus, they had a perspective on the case no one else shared. None of the observers coming to a judgment about the case can filter out what part of that judgment was based on the evidence and what part was based on things the jurors never heard.

Unfortunately, the O. J. verdict now carries the baggage of the public reaction to the verdict, divided along racial lines. That's not baggage the jurors are responsible for. In fact, they were instructed to ignore the potential public impact as a factor that should carry no weight in their deliberations.

One simple remedy proposed is that we throw away the blinders and no longer sequester juries. While we need to explore ways to modify sequestration to reduce the burdens and strains we place on jurors, we cannot abandon the effort to insulate jurors from all the extraneous factors that have no bearing on their task of resolving the facts based only on the evidence.

This brings me to lesson number 2: *bad journalism drives out the good*. A corollary of this is this: *journalism abhors a vacuum*. Many focused upon the television camera in the courtroom as the cause of

GERALD F. UELMEN

the media frenzy. I happen to agree that the television camera was a mistake because it affected the behavior of all the trial participants—judge, lawyers, and, most regrettably, witnesses. However, it was also the source of the discovery of significant evidence for both sides—an advantage that is often overlooked. The defense discovered Kathleen Bell, who witnessed Mark Fuhrman's racism firsthand, only after she saw Fuhrman testify on television and recognized him. The prosecution was the beneficiary of a bonanza of photos showing O. J. Simpson wearing gloves, sent in by helpful television viewers.

The television camera was not the worst culprit, however. Far worse were the tabloids who viewed the trial as a source of titillation and entertainment. When the trial began, I had a very clear idea of the difference between the tabloids and the legitimate press. As the trial progressed, that line became blurrier and blurrier. Just as the economists say bad money drives out the good, we saw bad journalism drive out the good—reporters tripping over one another to report every leak, giving credence to the wildest of rumors. At one point, when the *National Enquirer* ran a computer-simulated photo of a battered and bruised Nicole Brown Simpson, we asked, "Who would have ever thought the *National Enquirer* could stoop to the level of *Time* magazine?" (Time had enhanced a cover photo of O. J. to make him appear blacker.) One tabloid even ran a topless photo of prosecutor Marcia Clark, which they purchased from her obliging former mother-in-law.

Both the print and the television media demanded a steady supply of stories, even when there was nothing new to report. Marcia Clark's divorce filled the vacuum. When things really got slow, the press would do stories about one another to help hype the books many of them were writing.

The lawyers were not without blame in feeding this frenzy. But the remedy was not to simply gag the lawyers, as a new rule of professional conduct announced by the California Supreme Court does. Rather than accepting responsibility for public statements, lawyers now simply become the "informed sources" you see quoted without attribution. The reporters' shield law will protect them from exposure, and the public will be deprived of vital information to help them independently assess the credibility of news sources.

Hard lesson number 3 is *money makes a difference*, even when it comes to our justice system. This one is so obvious that I find it amusing that so many pundits seem shocked by it. We've long accepted the social reality that wealthy people eat better food, live in more comfortable houses, and get better medical care. Why does it surprise us that they get better representation in court? Why does it surprise us that a wealthy man would employ every resource available to him when his life or liberty is on the line? What's even more amusing is that the most vociferous criticism of the costly Simpson defense comes from conservatives who extol the virtues of free competition in a market economy in every other aspect of our lives.

The demonstration that access to the best lawyers and the best experts can make a difference in the outcome should cause us to take a hard look at the level of representation we provide to indigents accused of crime. There are still many places in America where a person on trial for his life is limited to a total budget that wouldn't have paid the hotel bill for one of the lawyers representing O. J. Simpson. Yet at the same time, some politicians seriously proposed that all criminals accused be limited to public defender representation, and Congress voted to cut off all funding for death penalty resource centers that sought to raise the level of competence of lawyers assigned to represent indigents in death penalty cases.

One virtue of an occasional defendant with the means to mount a well-financed defense is often overlooked. Like any other system, the criminal justice system has a tendency to relax when it isn't challenged. In California, 97 percent of criminal cases are disposed of without a trial. The evidence is never challenged. That may lead to carelessness, sloppiness, and worse. In San Francisco, a lab technician doing drug testing found that her tests were never challenged in court, so she simply started certifying that the seized materials were illegal drugs without doing any test at all. Her fraudulent test results produced over two hundred convictions before she was exposed. Hopefully, a defense like that mounted in Simpson will benefit thousands of other defendants by setting a higher, more demanding standard of performance for the Los Angeles County coroner's office, the LAPD Crime Laboratory, and LAPD homicide detectives.

Hard lesson number 4 is also a message for law enforcement: *garbage in is garbage out*. The scientific breakthroughs that brought us DNA technology place a very powerful tool in the hands of law enforcement. Like any technology, however, it's only as good as the people who operate it. The incredible sensitivity of new testing regimens brings with it a greatly enhanced risk of human error. At the outset of the O. J. trial, Marcia Clark told the jury that collecting specimens for blood testing was as easy as mopping up your kitchen with a sponge. Apparently, the LAPD actually believed that.

The kind of training and collection procedures needed to reduce the risks of contamination will increase the demand of law enforcement for more resources. The competition for scarce resources is already intense among all agencies that serve the public. Police departments that are hard put to keep gasoline in their patrol cars will be hard put to invest in new technology for their crime labs. Perhaps it's time for statewide consolidation of police laboratories, with statewide standards for training and qualification of technicians.

The fifth and final hard lesson is the most obvious of all: *racism is alive and well in America, and so is denial.* I was really struck by the difference in the reactions to the Fuhrman tapes that emanated from whites and blacks. Whites were shocked and surprised. Blacks simply shrugged their shoulders and said, "What's new?" After the verdict, I heard some whites say, "Thank goodness we don't live in Los Angeles."

It's time for a lot more candor and a lot less denial in assessing the role that race plays in our criminal justice system. We think we've made a lot of progress in race relations in America, but the criminal justice system demonstrates some alarming trends. One out of three black males under the age of twenty-five is either in jail or on probation or parole. That exceeds the number of young black males in college. Study after study verifies that color makes a difference at virtually every stage of the proceedings. Whites do better at getting charges dropped. They're better able to get charges reduced to lesser offenses. They draw more lenient sentences for the same crimes and go to prison less often. In California, blacks represent 7 percent of the population, but 35 percent of the prison population. That proportion increased dramatically as a result of the Three Strikes law. There are lots of explanations for this, including a war on drugs that promotes incarceration rather than treatment. It cannot be denied that the deployment of police resources has a disparate impact on minority communities. When you're on the receiving end, it's hard not to come to the conclusion that our justice system is far from color-blind.

Did O. J. Simpson take unfair advantage of the life experience of his jurors to persuade them that he was the victim of a police conspiracy? That's a fair question. Obviously, it should not be a defense to the crime of murder that the investigating detective used the N-word in the past ten years. But that characterization of the defense misses the point. The real point is that in denying and covering up the racism of Detective Fuhrman, he and other members of LAPD were exposed as liars who could not be trusted. Trust is what it's all about, and the first step in building trust is to be honest with each other. For me, the biggest disappointment in the public reaction to the verdict was the extent to which it revealed the deep distrust that divides black and white in America.

The hardest lessons from the O. J. trial are ultimately lessons about ourselves and one another: That we wear tinted lenses. That our appetite for gossip and scandal is what drives our mass media. That our appetite for money is what drives our economy, and what drives our economy is what drives our system of justice. That our sloppiness and carelessness cause injury to others. And that our ignorance and suspicion of one another causes pain.

---

*   From *Issues in Ethics*, Winter 1996 (Markkula Center for Applied Ethics)

3

Jury Bashing and the O. J. Simpson Verdict*

F ROM THE PERSPECTIVE of public opinion, the biggest loser in the trial of *People v. O. J. Simpson* was not the prosecution. It was not Judge Ito. It was the jury. Shortly after the trial, a survey in a judicial district in Los Angeles asked respondents to rate the performance of the various participants in the O. J. Simpson trial. The pool surveyed was very conservative. They identified themselves as 55 percent Republican, 59 percent "conservative," and 15 percent "very conservative." When asked whether they agreed or disagreed with the statement that California should make convicted criminals do manual labor in chain gangs, 74 percent expressed agreement. This is how those survey respondents rated the performance of the Simpson trial participants:

> Judge Ito: 70 percent good or excellent
> Marcia Clark: 79 percent good or excellent
> Johnnie Cochran: 58 percent good or excellent
> The jury: 30 percent good or excellent

These results demonstrate the perils befalling a jury that follows instructions. Following instructions has always been a perilous venture for a jury. There is an honorable and long tradition of jury bashing in American history. A dramatic example dates back to 1882 in Cincinnati. When a young stable hand who was put on trial for strangling his boss was found guilty of manslaughter instead of murder, there was a huge demonstration. A large crowd went to a music hall, where the judge of the superior court for that county in Ohio exhorted the assembled throng to drive from the community the jury that had returned that unpopular verdict, as well as the defense lawyer who had asked for it. The crowd then went to the jail, where they sought to lynch the defendant. They were driven away and then proceeded to burn down the courthouse. Then ensued a Cincinnati riot in which forty-five people were killed. A subsequent grand jury investigation looked into the incident, and the grand jury concluded the real fault did not lie with the judge who exhorted the crowd or with the newspapers that fanned the excitement. The real problem lay with the jury that returned a reprehensible verdict and with the defense lawyer who argued for it. A young assistant prosecutor then led an unsuccessful effort to get that lawyer disbarred. Incidentally, the name of that defense lawyer was Tom Campbell, and those riots in Cincinnati were known as the Tom Campbell riots. The young prosecutor who sought to get Tom Campbell disbarred was William Howard Taft, providing a wonderful example of how jury bashing and criminal defense lawyer bashing can lay the foundations for a spectacular political career. William Howard Taft served as the youngest solicitor general in American history and was appointed chief judge of the U.S. Court of Appeals for the Sixth Circuit at the age of thirty-five. After service as Theodore Roosevelt's secretary of war, he was elected president of the United States in 1908. He also served as chief justice of the United States from 1921 to 1930.

It is true that even defense lawyers occasionally join in and bash verdicts they don't agree with. For example, regarding the verdict in the first trial of the Menendez brothers for murdering their parents, Alan Dershowitz said, "What I am criticizing is the foolish juries who fall for the sob stories told by the lawyers" (*The Abuse Excuse* 28 [1994]). I myself have fallen prey to this temptation. After the first Rodney King verdict, acquitting the police officers whose vicious beating of King was captured on videotape, I wrote, "Apparently, it was easy to convince a jury of white suburbanites to disconnect their eyeballs from their brains and not be satisfied with seeing." Upon rereading those words, I was reminded of the Latin maxim *verba volant, scripta manent*: spoken words fly away, but written words remain to haunt you. Some may suggest that I lack standing to protest the bashing that the Simpson jury has taken because I have engaged in jury bashing myself. Nonetheless, I feel compelled to respond to some of the less-informed criticism of the Simpson jury.

GERALD F. UELMEN

In 1996 in California, we were treated to what has become a recurring spectacle: the unveiling of a new initiative measure to instantly cure all the ills of the criminal justice system. That year's initiative was called the Public Safety Protection Act of 1996, and its chief feature was the abolition of the requirement of unanimity in criminal jury trials. This initiative would have allowed a verdict to be returned by a vote of ten of the twelve jurors, except in death penalty cases. At the press conference announcing this new initiative, trotted out as the poster boy was Fred Goldman, the father of one of O. J.'s alleged victims. This was déjà vu for Californians because the poster boys for the "three strikes and you're out" initiative were the family of Polly Klaas. The Klaases later opposed the measure after realizing they were being used to promote a measure that did not really address the problem with which they were concerned. No one really explained the connection between Fred Goldman and a proposal to abolish unanimity in California jury trials. There also seemed to be little obvious connection to the Simpson trial. The chief criticism of the Simpson jury was that it did not deliberate long enough. If this measure had been in effect, the jury would have reached a verdict in ten minutes instead of four hours because the jury would not even have had to listen to the initial doubts of two of their fellow jurors after the first vote was taken. If we truly value deliberation, then we should seek to encourage jurors to listen to the concerns and doubts expressed by minority jurors rather than seeking to permit an instant verdict to be filed over the objections of two of the jurors.

The foregoing objection does not mean there was *no* connection between the Simpson case and this proposal. Indeed, there was a connection, but it was much more subtle. The connection was the growing power of minority jurors and the fear of that power by the white majority. That connection was made the day after the Simpson verdict was announced; it was made in the *Wall Street Journal*, which ran a lead story under the headline "Color Blinded." The story in question was not overtly a story about the O. J. Simpson verdict, but no one could read it without making the obvious connection. The story reported that race was playing an increasing role in jury verdicts around the country and that this phenomenon fit neatly into a tradition of political activism by U.S. juries. An acquittal rate of 47.6 percent for black defendants in the Bronx was attributed to the fact that juries there are 80 percent black.

The article concluded that this phenomenon may reflect an increase in "jury nullification" by black juries, reporting the following:

> Some jury nullification advocates now say blacks are justified in using their jury room vote to fight what they perceive as a national crisis: a justice system that is skewed against them by courts, prosecutors, and racist police such as former Los Angeles Detective Mark Fuhrman.

However, the verdict in the case of *People v. O. J. Simpson* was not jury nullification. Those who suggest it was simply have not listened to the jurors' explanation of their verdict. Shortly after the verdict, one of the jurors said "she thought O. J. 'probably did it,' but she understood that 'probably' wasn't good enough, that she had to be convinced beyond a reasonable doubt." What a wonderful affirmation that a juror could understand so clearly and follow so faithfully the instructions of the court. The verdict was a vindication of the principle that guilt must be proven beyond a reasonable doubt.

Now did the racial composition of the jury affect their assessment of reasonable doubt? Of course it did. Every defense lawyer knows that factors such as race, religion, gender, and life experience of the jurors will affect how they assess reasonable doubt; and those factors become especially important when assessing the credibility of police officers. No matter what color a client is, a defense lawyer working on a case involving police perjury will want as many black jurors as possible, and the prosecution will want as many white jurors as possible. That is not jury nullification—it is common sense. Similarly, the verdict of the Simi Valley jurors in the Rodney King beating case was not white jury nullification. It was simply white reasonable doubt.

This argument may lead some to conclude that lawyers should not be allowed to affect the racial composition of juries by means of peremptory challenges (i.e., that we should abolish peremptory challenges). That argument is worth discussing, but it has little to do with the Simpson case. What is frequently overlooked about the Simpson case is that when both sides stood up and announced that they accepted the jury that had been selected, neither side had exercised all its peremptory challenges. The prosecution had exercised only ten of its twenty peremptory challenges, although it had used eight of those ten challenges to excuse African American jurors. The defense had exercised

GERALD F. UELMEN

only nine of its twenty peremptory challenges—excusing five whites, one African American, one Hispanic, and two Native Americans.

The diversity of the Simpson jury had nothing to do with peremptory challenges or with the use of jury consultants, for that matter. It had more to do with where the trial was held. The most vigorous criticism of the Los Angeles County district attorney in the wake of the Simpson verdict attacked his failure to move the trial to Santa Monica or the San Fernando Valley, where the jury would have been less diverse. Interestingly, his predecessor as district attorney was criticized precisely because he did move the Rodney King case to the Simi Valley. But gerrymandering a trial's location to affect the racial composition is not called "playing a race card" in Los Angeles.

It is also interesting that the supreme court ruling in *Batson v. Kentucky*—that lawyers must offer nondiscriminatory explanations for a pattern of excusing minority jurors—really has little impact on the prosecutorial use of race as a factor in jury selection, and it will have even less effect after a subsequent ruling that the explanation for the prosecutor's peremptory challenge does not even have to be a plausible explanation. Any prosecutor with a little imagination can come up with a race-neutral reason for striking a black juror. The prize ought to go to the Virginia prosecutor who, when asked to explain why he excused an African American man, explained that it was because the man showed evidence of an undesirable "sympathetic disposition." The evidence was the fact that he was wearing a crucifix around his neck, and the Virginia Supreme Court upheld that as a race-neutral explanation for the exercise of a peremptory challenge.

Is the solution to all this simply to abolish peremptory challenges? If we could come up with a uniform and fair system of challenges for cause, an abolition of peremptory challenges would be an improvement. The problem is that most judges apply a ludicrous standard in a challenge for cause. They simply let the jurors themselves be the final arbiter of whether or not they are biased. For example, some judges conducted voir dire examinations by walking into the courtroom and asking, "Are any of you here biased against African Americans? If you are, would you please raise your hand?"

In a recent Louisiana Supreme Court decision, the court held that a judge was not required to excuse for cause a juror who had gone to the funeral home to visit the murder victim's body and who was employed as a prison guard because she assured the trial court of her impartiality. In another case, a North Carolina judge allowed a prosecutor to sit on a jury despite the fact that he worked in the same DA's office as the prosecutor trying the case because he told the judge he could overcome the difficulty of remaining objective. If this kind of standard is applied in challenges for cause, peremptory challenges are needed as a safety valve to ensure that biased jurors are actually excused from sitting on juries.

Americans are free to accept or reject the verdict of any jury and apparently felt no reluctance to do so in the case of *People v. O. J. Simpson*. But disagreement with a verdict rendered in good faith by those who patiently sat and listened to all the evidence does not justify publicly bashing the jurors and accusing them of being racists or ignoramuses. If anything will discourage citizens from responding to a summons to perform their civic duty to serve on juries, it is the prospect of their fellow citizens engaging in the American sport of jury bashing.

---

*   From *Harvard Journal of Law & Public Policy*, vol. 20, p. 476 (1996–1997)

4

Lizzie Borden Meets
O. J. Simpson

WHEN JUDGE GEORGE Choppelas, who presided over the lunchtime entertainment of the San Francisco Court of Historical Inquiry, called and invited me to represent Lizzie Borden in a mock retrial, I was vaguely aware of the parallels between Lizzie's "trial of the century" and the "trial of the century" in which I had recently participated, the case of *People v. O. J. Simpson*. ("Trial of the century" may be a bit of overused hyperbole. I've located thirty-four trials in the twentieth century that were labeled the "trial of the century" or "the crime of the century." We have a trial of the century every three years.)

I knew that Lizzie, like O. J., had been quickly acquitted by a jury and that much of the public generally rejected that verdict and concluded she was guilty anyhow. Lizzie became a social pariah, taunted by the children's rhyme that inaccurately tallied the whacks she allegedly administered to the heads of her family. The rhyme is a classic example of media exaggeration. If Lizzie was indeed the perpetrator, she didn't give "her mother 40 whacks." It was her stepmother, and the coroner found nineteen wounds. And her father was the recipient of fourteen whacks, not forty-one.

What I did not realize until I delved into the historical accounts of Lizzie's trial was that the trial of O. J Simpson was a historical replay that eerily resembled the Borden trial in dozens of particulars. The defense theory in both cases was precisely the same: The perpetrator of two very bloody murders would have been drenched in blood. Where was the bloody clothing Lizzie wore? Where was the bloody hatchet? There seemed to be just as many theories of how Lizzie disposed of her hatchet and her dress as there were to explain how O. J. supposedly dumped his clothing and shoes and got rid of a knife. In both cases, however, the prosecution could produce little evidence to back up the theories. In Lizzie's case, the prosecutors argued that Lizzie had casually burned the bloody dress in the presence of two witnesses two days after the murders. The defense had a very plausible explanation: that Lizzie was disposing of a paint-stained garment, naively giving no thought whatsoever to the possibility of incriminating inferences that might be drawn.

In O. J.'s case, the police expended enormous efforts in searching the waste containers of dozens of airplanes, searching the fields surrounding a Chicago hotel, and finally suggesting that the evidence was neatly packed in a carry-on bag that disappeared into the ethereal cosmos. When the barn behind Lizzie's house was torn down years ago, the remains were carefully sifted in an effort to locate the missing axe. The Borden family home in Fall River, Massachusetts, was recently opened as a bed-and-breakfast establishment. Thousands of tourists will now explore every crevice, still looking for a bloody axe. If they ever convert O. J.'s Rockingham mansion into a hotel, they should preserve the white carpets that lead all the way up the stairs to the master bedroom. Guests can marvel at the mystery of how a blood-drenched murderer made his way up those stairs without leaving a droplet of blood on the carpet. (Note: the Rockingham mansion was bulldozed by the new owner in 1998).

In our mock retrial of Lizzie, the prosecutors offered the explanation that Lizzie removed her clothing and committed the murders in the nude! Actually, this implausible scenario was not original. In a 1975 Emmy Award–winning television movie titled *The Legend of Lizzie Borden*, Paramount Television portrayed Lizzie removing her clothing, axing her stepmother, cleaning up and dressing again to greet her father, then repeating the strip and wash before dropping the bloody axe down the basement privy. But even in 1892, police had enough sense (and enough stamina) to search the privy.

It's a safe bet that when Hollywood does *The Legend of O. J. Simpson*, they'll depict O. J. driving up to Rockingham in his boxer shorts. The most remarkable parallel between the cases of Lizzie Borden and O. J. Simpson, however, was in the role that the American media played in both trials. The media coverage of the O. J. trial was a remarkable demonstration of the principle that bad journalism drives out good. The traditional line between the "legitimate" press and the "tabloid" press became a very blurry one, with the *National Enquirer* and Geraldo Rivera setting the pace.

When selecting the jury, the O. J. defense discovered an interesting phenomenon. The media coverage was so excessive, tasteless, and speculative that rather than prejudicing jurors, it made them into skeptics. Defense lawyers prefer jurors who are skeptical of "official explanations." The media circus actually benefitted the defense because so much was exposed as nonsense before the trial began. Remarkably, that is precisely what happened in the case of *Commonwealth v. Lizzie Borden*. Back then, most Americans got their news from newspapers rather than television, and most American newspapers of the day were in fact tabloids without pictures. They paid cash for their stories, and to the newspaper reporters and editors of a century ago, public interest and prurient interest meant the same thing.

The October 10, 1892, issue of the *Boston Globe* appeared two months after the murders while Lizzie was in custody awaiting trial. Lizzie's trial did not begin until a year after the murders, so the media frenzy had even more time to build. As "trials of the century" go, O. J. actually set a record for the speed with which the case was prepared for trial. The trial began only four months after the murders. The front page of the October 10, 1892, *Boston Globe* screamed "Lizzie Had a Secret!" Claiming that the newspaper had gained access to investigative reports of the statements of twenty-five witnesses, the *Globe* reported that Lizzie was pregnant and that her embarrassing predicament led to a violent confrontation with her father. The newspaper exulted in its "scoop," making the widespread public amazement at its revelations into a follow-up story, with the self-congratulatory headline "Police Think the Scoop Is a Corker!" The "scoop," it turned out, was the product of the fervid imagination of a detective employed by the police who received $1,000 in cash for delivering the "witness statements" to newspaper reporter Henry Trickey. Trickey was a remarkable character, only twenty-four years old and already a top reporter for one of the leading newspapers in the country. In one of the more bizarre twists of Lizzie Borden's case, the same grand jury that returned her indictment for murder on December 2, 1892, returned a second indictment of reporter Henry Trickey for tampering with witnesses. Three days after his indictment, Trickey died under the wheels of a train in Ontario, Canada, an apparent suicide.

Many historians of the Lizzie Borden case conclude that the media excess actually worked in Lizzie's favor because the jury was quite sympathetic to her defense after seeing so much of the media coverage exposed as malicious lies. I'm personally convinced a similar phenomenon was at work in O. J.'s case. At least in the black community, the blatant racism that pervaded coverage of the case by national newsmagazines like *Time* and *Newsweek* made a claim that racist police-planted evidence much more plausible. It should not be assumed that massive pretrial publicity will inevitably disadvantage a defendant. One poll revealed the extent to which Americans are becoming more skeptical of the media. In 1997, more than half, 56 percent, of Americans reported an opinion that the media frequently gets the story wrong compared to only 45 percent who reported such an opinion ten years before.

The media frenzy surrounding trials like Lizzie Borden's and O. J. Simpson's has a very seductive influence on ordinary people who want to achieve some sort of notoriety. One of the most difficult tasks facing both the lawyers and the journalists is sorting out the nutcases from the legitimate witnesses. The difference is not always obvious. In Lizzie's case, both police and news reporters were plagued with stories of "sightings" of the perpetrator in the vicinity of Fall River on the day of the murders. Andrew Borden's reputation as a stingy and selfish skinflint helped fuel the stories, which suggested as possible suspects dozens of former employees or business associates who might have had a motive to do him in. Similarly, the lifestyle of Nicole Brown Simpson did not permit one to quickly dismiss all the claims of sightings of suspicious characters lurking about the premises on the night in question. One of the most bizarre "eyewitnesses" to emerge was a man who claimed to be standing at an intersection halfway between the Bundy crime scene and O. J.'s residence at 10:30 p.m. the night of the murders. He said he observed a white Bronco screech to a halt, narrowly avoiding an accident. He saw a person on the opposite curb wave and exclaim, "Hey, O. J.!" And he had the presence of mind to note the license number as the Bronco sped away. The only reason he did not appear as a star witness at the trial was that the license number he produced was the license number of Al Cowlings's Bronco, which everyone saw on television during the slow-speed chase.

Another remarkable replay of Lizzie's trial occurred when a guard at the jail where O. J. was in custody volunteered that he "overheard" an incriminating conversation between O. J. and Roosevelt Grier, the football great turned minister, who was offering spiritual counseling to O. J. While Lizzie was awaiting trial in custody, a local sheriff actually hid himself under her bed so he could listen to her conversations with visitors. In O. J.'s case, the court ruled that the guard could not testify because of the assurances given to Simpson that arrangements for him to confer with his lawyers and minister were secure. The prosecution in Lizzie's case never even offered the jail snoop as a witness, concluding what he had to offer was not worth risking the indignation a jury would feel toward such ungentlemanly conduct.

It took four hours to pick the jury in the Lizzie Borden case. In the O. J. trial, it took two months. But even here, there was a strong parallel. In Lizzie's day, the jurors were all male and, of course, all white. It doesn't take a sophisticated jury consultant to figure out that a jury of males would be to Lizzie's advantage. That advantage was a given; the prosecutors could do nothing to control the gender of the jurors. While much has been written about the "race cards" being played in the selection of the O. J. jury, it turns out that "gender" cards were just as important. Sophisticated jury experts were consulted, and they suggested that a jury of females would be to O. J.'s advantage. The exercise of peremptory challenges by both sides reflected this reality, with the defense less inclined to accept males and the prosecution less inclined to accept females.

The Lizzie Borden jury returned a verdict in one hour and six minutes. The jury in *People v. O. J. Simpson* was widely criticized for reaching a verdict too quickly—in four hours. Although the Borden verdict was controversial, I have never read one word of criticism of the jurors. Jury bashing was not unknown in the nineteenth century, but by and large, Americans were much more willing to accept the verdict of a jury. Even though Lizzie was treated like a pariah, her jurors were never subjected to the vicious sniping directed at the O. J. jury. The phenomenon of jury bashing, at least to the extent we now practice it, is certainly related to television coverage of trials. By creating the illusion that we all know just as much about the case as the jurors, television creates a license to substitute our judgment for theirs. Another thing that has apparently changed is the willingness of lawyers to join in. The extent to which prosecutors have made the judge and jury the scapegoats for their ineptitude has certainly contributed to the growing popularity of the American sport of jury bashing.

Just like the O. J. case, Lizzie Borden's case turned many of the judges and lawyers into celebrities. One of the more fascinating comparisons between the two cases is to look at what their celebrity did for the lawyers and judges in the two cases and, perhaps a more profound question, what they did with their celebrity. In Lizzie's case, there was actually a panel of three judges presiding, so there was a collaborative process and collective responsibility that Judge Lance Ito might have welcomed in the O. J. trial. Lizzie's was actually the first case tried under a Massachusetts statute requiring a three-judge panel for capital cases, which went into effect in 1891. (Massachusetts has since abolished the death penalty.) For all three judges, Lizzie's was the most spectacular case of otherwise-unremarkable careers. All three ended their judicial careers in the same positions they occupied at the time of the Borden trial. Then, as it is now, presiding over a high-profile trial was not the way to advance a judicial career. Even though they lost the case, both of Lizzie's prosecutors went on to spectacular political careers. Hosea Knowlton was elected Massachusetts attorney general in the next election. William Moody was elected to Congress and later served as Theodore Roosevelt's attorney general. He ended his career as a justice of the U.S. Supreme Court. Gil Garcetti, on the other hand, was nearly unseated as Los Angeles County district attorney after the O. J. trial.

Lizzie's defense lawyers, who were both very talented trial lawyers, were also ambitious politicians. Andrew Jennings was elected district attorney in the next election, to succeed Hosea Knowlton. George Robinson was already in the twilight of a successful political career. He had been elected to Congress and served three terms as the governor of Massachusetts. He had even appointed one of Lizzie's judges to the bench. So of course, he was regarded by the judges as a lawyer of eminent wisdom! One benefit the Lizzie Borden case brought him was that it certainly made him richer. He received a fee of $25,000 for his services, which would translate to a cool million in today's dollars.

It's interesting that the O. J. lawyers and judges are seeing significantly different effects on their careers from their notoriety. Judge Ito may never recover. The judge who awarded O. J. custody of his children faced the threat of a recall election. The obvious lesson for judges is to keep your head down if you want to rise. Some of the O.

J. lawyers have parlayed their celebrity into media careers: book deals, television contracts, and a plethora of movies yet to come. Thus, the line between the practice of law and a career in show business also became somewhat blurry in the wake of the O. J. trial. None of the participants in Lizzie's trial ever wrote a book about it. It can almost be said that none of the participants in O. J.'s trial did not write a book about it. Having written two of them and read all of them, I can offer one reflection. Every book probably revealed more about its author than it did about the trial. I had to keep asking myself as I read each book, "Were we at the same trial?"

Both the trials of Lizzie Borden and O. J. Simpson offer more lessons about American culture than they do about our system of justice. Neither can be understood except as a uniquely American cultural event. Perhaps the most profound lesson they teach us about American culture is our immutable inability to ever learn anything from our past. We pride ourselves on how far we've come in the past century, but our "trials of the century" tell us that we like to keep doing everything the same way.

My real claim to fame from the Simpson trial arose from my role as poet laureate of the defense team. I proudly claim full credit for feeding Johnnie Cochran the line "If it doesn't fit, you must acquit." Thus, in defending Lizzie Borden in our mock retrial, I again sought poetic justice. After all, in judging Lizzie, the American people apparently put more credence in a snappy jingle than they did in the jury's verdict. So let me close with the same couplet that I recited to our jury in the Lizzie retrial by the San Francisco Court of Historical Inquiry:

Without an axe or bloodstained dress,
Lizzie's not a murderess.
Rather than the criminal type,
She's just a victim of media hype.
So put aside the childish rhyme
That links her name with brutal crime.
Accept, without a doubt or worry,
The verdict of an American jury.

More than one hundred years after her original trial, Lizzie was once again acquitted.

---

*   From *LITIGATION*, State Bar of California, Winter 1998, vol. 24, no. 2, p. 59.

Race Cards: Good Lawyers as Bad Citizens*

SHORTLY AFTER JOHNNIE Cochran's spellbinding final summation in the case of *People v. Simpson*, nationally syndicated columnist George Will wrote that Cochran was a "good lawyer," but a "bad citizen" (George F. Will, "Circus of the Century," *Washington Post*, October 4, 1995, p. A25.) In context, he was reflecting upon Cochran's argument that Detective Mark Fuhrman should be disbelieved because of his virulent racist attitude. He was asserting that the argument would stir up racial resentments and set back race relations in the United States, as well as diminish respect for the police.

Will's criticism called to mind the criticism heaped upon another great advocate more than a century ago. Henry Lord Brougham was representing Queen Caroline of England in proceedings before Parliament. King George IV, who had just succeeded to the Crown, was seeking to divorce his wife, Queen Caroline, on grounds of her adultery. Parliament was considering a special bill that would deprive the queen of her title. At that time, English law permitted a "right of recrimination" as a defense to a divorce action. If Lord Brougham could show that the king himself had engaged in adulterous affairs, grounds for a divorce would disappear. It was certainly the British "trial of the century" for 1820. Lord Brougham not only had substantial evidence of the king's affairs with numerous women, but also showed that, while Prince of Wales, George had secretly married one of his mistresses, a Roman Catholic widow named Maria Fitzherbert. At that time, marriage to a Catholic meant forfeiture of the Crown for a British sovereign. By invoking the right of recrimination for his client, Lord Brougham provoked a constitutional crisis of the greatest magnitude. His advocacy on behalf of his client threatened to bring the reign of

King George IV to an ignominious end before the king had even been crowned. Many suggested to Lord Brougham that his duty to be a good citizen and promote the welfare of his country required him to "pull his punches" and not assert the right of recrimination against the king. Generations of lawyers who followed after Lord Brougham have pointed to his response as the quintessential definition of the appropriate role of a defense lawyer:

> An advocate, in the discharge of his duty, knows but one person in all the world, and that person is his client. To save that client by all means and expedients, and at all hazards and costs to other persons, and, amongst them, to himself, is his first and only duty; and in performing this duty he must not regard the alarm, the torments, the destruction which he may bring upon others. Separating the duty of a patriot from that of an advocate, he must go on reckless of consequences, though it should be his unhappy fate to involve his country in confusion.

Today, there are some who argue that Lord Brougham was guilty of overstating the case. Prominent British barrister David Pannick, in his highly regarded book *Advocates*, suggests that "such a conception of the role of the advocate would not now be widely shared. [An advocate] has important responsibilities to the court as well as to his client." The late chief justice Warren Burger, also critical of Lord Brougham's model, rebuked "cynics who view the lawyer much as the 'hired gun' of the Old West." I do not believe that either Mr. Pannick or Chief Justice Burger would suggest that Lord Brougham should not have asserted the right of recrimination in Queen Caroline's case despite the national confusion it engendered. Nor do I believe any knowledgeable lawyer would suggest that Johnnie Cochran should not have utilized the evidence of Detective Mark Fuhrman's racism to challenge his credibility because it would increase racial tensions in the United States. The critiques of Lord Brougham's bromide generally focus on his suggestion that saving one's client is the lawyer's only duty.

Clearly, a lawyer has duties to others as well. A lawyer's duties to the court preclude the knowing presentation of perjured testimony and the intentional nondisclosure of controlling authority rejecting a legal position one is arguing. A California lawyer also has substantial duties imposed by the reciprocal discovery law to provide opposing counsel with evidence in advance of its presentation at trial. But do the lawyer's duties to others include a duty to be a "good citizen" and not assert arguments or present evidence that will "involve the country in confusion"?

It seems fair to say that the successful defense of O. J. Simpson has indeed "involved our country in confusion." The trial has been credited with setting back race relations, lowering public esteem for the legal profession, diminishing respect for the police, and destroying public confidence in the criminal justice system. While some of these effects might reasonably have been anticipated, should they have been considered and weighed by the lawyers in assessing what tactical options to pursue? Should lawyers ever abandon an argument or fail to present evidence that will help their client because it will hurt their country? The suggestion that lawyers owe a higher duty to their country than to their client is inconsistent with our adversary system, although it was quite commonly heard in communist countries that rejected the adversary system. In such communist systems, lawyers are seen as servants of the state rather than as advocates for their clients. The premise of the adversary system is that the goal of fair adjudication is more likely to be served if lawyers function as zealous advocates for their clients and leave judgments about what is good for the "system" for another time and place. Thus, lawyers who serve their clients are, by definition, serving their country as well. The duty of lawyers to their clients and their country is the same: "to represent [the] client zealously within the bounds of the law."

I would take this position a step beyond simply rejecting the suggestion that lawyers owe some higher duty to their country. I would argue that it would be unethical for a lawyer who felt some higher duty to act upon it to the detriment of the client. Any lawyer who decides what evidence to offer or what positions to assert in a criminal case based upon considerations such as "Will this advance the goal of racial equality?" or "Will this lessen public confidence in the justice system?" is cheating the client. In effect, the lawyer has created a conflict of interest. The lawyer who has personal objections to asserting the cause of the client because of a perception that the cause of the nation is more important has only one choice: to resign.

This is not to say that such considerations are irrelevant to the client. A lawyer can, and probably should, advise a client that a particular position or argument may hurt the best interests of the country. The choice of whether to forgo the advantage, however, must be left to the client. In a criminal case, where the life or liberty of the client is at stake, it will be a rather unusual client who will say, "I'd rather go to jail—or be gassed or electrocuted—than imperil the interests of my country."

Thus, calling a good lawyer a bad citizen is internally inconsistent. By being a good lawyer who zealously represents the interests of a client, the lawyer is being a good citizen who preserves the tenets of our adversary system of justice. Obviously, this is not a proposition that the public understands or applauds. When Lord Brougham referred to the hazards and costs to oneself that a lawyer may incur, he certainly included the hazard and cost of public unpopularity. A lawyer who, in pursuit of the obligation to zealously represent a client, asserts positions that are publicly perceived as disturbing to the nation's tranquility will receive the opprobrium of fellow citizens. In the eyes of the public, it will not be accepted as an excuse or justification that the lawyer was only doing the job ethically required. That is simply a risk a lawyer must accept when choosing to represent the client. The lawyers who represented O. J. Simpson, including myself, have all been treated to public castigation with a steady diet of "hate mail" and personal threats to their safety. The real problem is not the role of the lawyer, but rather the public misunderstanding of that role. One of the duties of good citizens should be to promote public understanding rather than public confusion. In that respect, it can truly be said that George Will is a good columnist, but a bad citizen.

---

* From *Loyola of Los Angeles Law Review*, vol. 30, p. 119 (1996–1997).

6

Ruminations on the Lessons of O. J.

I TITLED ONE of my books about the O. J. trial *Lessons from the Trial*. I did not characterize the lessons to be learned as ways we could "fix the system." The failures in our system of justice are not, for the most part, systemic failures. We have a sound system—if we let it do its work. The failures are mostly operative failures, in which those we trust to operate the system fall short. The lessons I offered were lessons about human frailty and arrogance, motivation and struggle, competition and civility, and basic human dignity. "They are lessons about how bizarre and distorted things appear when they are magnified and exaggerated. They are lessons about how things that appear black and white are frequently gray."

Looking back on it all today, I'm disappointed at how little has changed. Advances in technology and communication enhance our ability to experience events as they happen and provide opportunities to "twitter" about what is happening as it happens. Unfortunately, these advances only magnify the human foibles that distorted the events of the O. J. trial. The pace of the "rush to judgment" has only been hastened.

We have actually increased the frequency of our "trials of the century." We now seem to have a new one every year. And like the O. J. trial, many of them are tinged with racism. Exposing the tenacity of racism still receives the dismissive "playing a race card" of Robert Shapiro. We need to get past the denial and recognize that the influence of racism remains embedded in American culture. The election of a black president did not put it behind us.

The O. J. trial did make one positive contribution to American awareness, however, and that was the frequency of domestic violence by professional athletes. The uneasy concurrence of professional violence on the football field and domestic violence off it is finally getting the attention it deserves. Police and prosecutors have shed the reluctance that once characterized the use of criminal sanctions in the face of uncooperative victims. The imposition of noncriminal remedies like suspension of athletes and forfeiture of compensation might have greater deterrent value.

In teaching my course in evidence, I raise serious objections to new rules of evidence that were enacted in the wake of the O. J. trial. Whenever a defendant is accused of domestic violence in California, all prior instances of domestic violence become admissible as evidence of his or her "propensity." Out-of-court hearsay statements, not subject to cross-examination, are regularly admitted when the out-of-court declarant was an alleged victim of domestic violence. These changes make it easier to convict someone who is accused of domestic violence, but the ease with which convictions are obtained does not seem to stem the tide of domestic violence. Most of it is rooted in abuse of alcohol and drugs. Reliance upon our criminal justice system as the first line of defense against domestic violence, however, is misplaced. Other alternatives may offer greater prospects for success.

In one post-trial interview, I was asked if there was anyone I would not defend. I clumsily explained that that a lawyer should not defend a client if he or she cannot defend with vigor, and I would have difficulty working up the necessary vigor to defend a purveyor of hate, to uphold the rights of an admitted Klansman or Nazi to promulgate their venom. While I admire the ACLU for stepping up to the plate in cases of this nature, it would not be a task I personally could perform with vigor. I was taken aback by the interviewer's next question: "You mean you will not defend marchers, but you will defend slashing someone's throat with a knife?" I was surprised by the question because I never conceived of what I was doing in the Simpson case as defending the *act* of murder. I was defending the liberty of a person who was *accused* of the crime of murder, not the crime itself. I would not defend the act of murder any more than I would defend words of hate. No one has the "right" to kill, and while we do recognize a right to utter words of hate, I would not choose to defend that right. In the public mind, this distinction is too subtle, and criminal defense lawyers regularly become the objects of the same public scorn directed at their clients.

Many of the most violent crimes we encounter today are crimes of hate, committed by terrorists who select their victims at random. I must confess to a sense of relief when the terrorists are killed by the police or end their reign of terror with suicide. The thought, for example, of bringing Osama bin Laden back to the United State to stand trial was especially abhorrent. The use of drones to eliminate terrorists is condemned by many of my liberal friends, but not by me as long as reasonable measures are taken to avoid taking out innocent bystanders along with them. Terrorists have declared war on us, and in fighting their war, the Geneva Conventions are simply not a factor in their planning. In preventing their attacks, we should be allowed to utilize the weapons of war. When a terrorist is captured and put on trial, I do not envy the courageous lawyers who step up to the plate to provide a defense. A trial could not be held without someone to perform that role. They deserve admiration rather than scorn. They are not defending terrorism; they are defending the Bill of Rights, which will be available to the best of us only when it remains available to the worst of us.

Ultimately, I must confess I enjoyed much of the media attention that gave me my "fifteen minutes of fame." I will never forget the exhilaration I felt when, after waiting in a long line of motorists crossing the Golden Gate Bridge, I pulled up to the toll booth, and as I handed over the toll, the attendant looked at me and said, "You were one of O. J.'s attorneys!" It's nice to be recognized. But being turned into an instant celebrity has its risks, and I will always be grateful to my wife and children for keeping me grounded and reminding me of what is most important in life—to love.

II

Ethics, Love, and the Search for Justice

1

The Conscience of a Criminal Defense Lawyer*

I N ONE OF my more cynical moments, I composed a poem that briefly sums up what most lawyers do:
Black may be gray. White may be gray.
When things are gray, they can go either way.
Painting things gray can pay.

If one of our goals in life is to find the truth and if a trial is supposed to be a search for the truth, how can a life painting things gray be a virtuous life? I regard the search for truth as one of the ultimate goals of life itself. I certainly seek truth in the library, at the dinner table, in the classroom, and in the chapel. I strive to keep truth at the core of my relationships with my family and friends, my students, and my professional colleagues. But here I come to dispute the notion that the ultimate purpose of a trial is to find the truth.

At the outset of a trial, we frequently encounter contrasting versions of what actually happened. The Oscar Pistorius case in South Africa provides a good example. The prosecutor said it was premeditated murder. The defendant said it was an unfortunate accident. The adversary system requires both the prosecution and the defense to pursue their versions relentlessly, with every tool of persuasion the law allows. Neither version is favored, although the defense version must prevail if the prosecution does not meet its burden of proof. Regardless of how convinced an advocate may be that the story he or she is presenting to the jury coincides with objective reality, it must remain a story until the jury has spoken. But the jury's verdict will simply be "guilty" or "not guilty." Does a "guilty" verdict establish the truth of the prosecution's version? Does a "not guilty" verdict establish the truth of the defense version? I submit that it does not. Those who believe that a trial should end with trumpets blaring and curtains parting as the jury announces "the truth" are deluding themselves. What we seek in a trial is simply an acceptable level of certainty, not a declaration of where the truth lies.

Our pursuit of the truth in a court of law must occasionally be tempered to respect the boundaries that civilized society has erected so we can live peaceably with one another. We are not entitled to unreasonably invade the privacy of others, even when we are convinced that such a mission will lead us to the truth. Respect for the autonomy of others requires that we concede their right to remain silent, even when we're sure that their words would illuminate our search for the truth. Respect for the sanctity of relationships requires we honor the privileges for communications between husband and wife, attorney and client, doctor and patient, and clergyman and penitent, even when revealing those communications might get us closer to the truth.

Thus, if we speak of a trial as a search for the truth, we must recognize that the search is subject to restraints that may ultimately affect the outcome. There are places we can't look. There are things we pretend not to see. Does that mean that the outcome is no longer the truth?

Even those who say a trial is a search for the truth must admit we don't always succeed in finding it. We tolerate a high margin of error to accommodate other goals. But this is misleading. A result in conformity with our goals should not be labeled an error. It may be better to say that the search for the truth has a unique meaning in the context of an adversary trial. While a trial is a contest between two versions of the facts, *neither* version may coincide with objective reality. At the conclusion of the trial, the jury is empowered to choose between the competing versions. The choice the jury makes does not define the truth. Actually, that choice has a very limited purpose. In a criminal trial, the purpose is to define the power of the state to punish an individual by depriving him of his life or liberty. In a civil trial, the purpose is simply to transfer money from one pocket to another. Conceivably, the same events can produce two results that appear inconsistent. That's precisely what happened in the O. J. trials. The state could not punish O. J. because he had been found not guilty, but the victims could recover a judgment requiring him to pay damages because he was found liable. That does not mean that either conclusion was wrong or erroneous. It simply reflects the differing levels of certainty we demand before a verdict can be rendered. Because we value liberty more than property, we require a higher threshold of certainty in a criminal trial. The defendant must be proven guilty beyond a reasonable doubt. Where only money is at stake, proof by a preponderance of the evidence is sufficient.

When we look at a trial from this perspective, it is more accurate to describe the trial as a search for certainty rather than a search for the truth. Certainty can be quantified, while truth cannot. Truth is absolute. Even absolute certainty does not define the truth. Truth should never be confused with certitude. The fact that a belief or conviction is universally shared does not make it the truth. At one time, nearly every person on earth believed that the sun revolved around the earth. That belief was confirmed by their own eyes. They observed the sun rising and setting each day. They concluded, "As far as I can see, the sun circles the earth." They just didn't realize how limited their vision was. The "trial of the century" of 1633 was the heresy trial of Galileo Galilei for teaching that the earth revolved around the sun. He was convicted. While his conviction of heresy vindicated conventional wisdom, it certainly didn't vindicate the truth.

If we conceive of a trial as a quest for certainty, should it not be an equal contest in which each side has the same opportunity to challenge the credibility of the other side's evidence? The credibility of the evidence should be the ultimate criterion of success. Here again, just as we distinguish between civil and criminal trials in quantifying the level of certainty required for a verdict, we recognize an essential difference in the restraints we impose on the adversaries. In a criminal trial, one of the adversaries is the state. The individual, regardless of how wealthy or powerful he may be, can never match the resources or power of the state itself. This disparity demands that we give the accused an advantage to start with. That advantage is called the "presumption of innocence." Literally, that means we have tilted the balance toward the version offered by the accused: that he is not guilty. The burden is upon the state to convince the jury of its version. The defendant does not have to offer any evidence at all. If the state falls short in meeting its burden, the defendant walks free. In a civil trial, however, there is no presumption. The party who presents the preponderance of the evidence will win.

There are many good reasons for the presumption of innocence, but the strongest reason is that we distrust the awesome power of the state. Is that distrust obsolete? In a democracy, the state is no longer an autocratic king, but our elected representatives. The lawyers who represent the state are honest, decent people who often accept lower salaries in order to serve the public. Why should their version be subjected to any greater burden than the version presented by the paid adversaries of an accused criminal?

For us, that question was answered resoundingly two centuries ago, when we amended our Constitution with a Bill of Rights. Those who created our form of democratic government were vigilant in recognizing the need to limit the power of government over individuals. The ensuring two centuries can hardly be cited as evidence that we no longer need to be vigilant, that we can now trust those who hold power.

That brings me to the question so often asked of criminal defense lawyers: "How can you defend someone when you know he's guilty?" I've never had to defend a client I "knew" was guilty because I never assumed the role of judging their guilt or innocence. In a criminal trial, that role is assigned to others. My role is to zealously assert and defend my client's best interest and to vigorously dispute and challenge the prosecution's case. Defense lawyers are obligated to give the same vigorous defense to a client they believe is guilty as to one they believe is innocent. Their personal belief is irrelevant, and in fact, they are prohibited from arguing their personal belief to the jury.

Both defense lawyers and prosecutors are subject to two important ethical constraints, however. Neither can knowingly participate in the presentation of perjured testimony. And neither can actively hide or suppress relevant evidence, making it unavailable to the other side. If a defense lawyer "knows" his client is guilty, presumably because his client has reliably told him so, he cannot assist that client in taking the witness stand and denying his guilt. Just as a prosecutor cannot assist a police officer in lying about the grounds he had to seize evidence if he "knows" the officer is lying.

The suppression by the prosecution of evidence favorable to an accused violates due process where the evidence is material either to guilt or punishment, irrespective of the good faith or bad faith of the prosecution. Violation of this duty can not only invalidate a conviction, but also lead to disciplinary action against the prosecutor.

Unfortunately, such violations are rarely exposed because the suppressed evidence remains buried in police or prosecution files that are not available to the defense.

Defense lawyers, on the other hand, are not required to disclose unfavorable evidence, although they are not permitted to conceal it. I use a very simple hypothetical to illustrate the difference for my students. I bring a toy gun in a paper sack into the classroom and tell the students, "Your client just walked into your office and said, 'I shot my wife, and here's the gun I used to do it.'" Then I place the bag in front of a squirming student and ask him or her what should be done with it. There are two acceptable answers to this question: One is you pick up the bag and place it in your desk drawer. If you do that, however, you will have to turn the gun over to the police or prosecutor. The other is to tell your client, "You keep it. You don't have to turn it over to the police. If I take it, I will." After tormenting my students with this dilemma, I found myself actually facing it during the O. J. case. The same day I flew to Los Angeles to join the defense team, the *National Enquirer* ran a front-page story revealing that three weeks before the murders, O. J. had walked into a cutlery store and purchased a nine-inch folding stiletto knife. They even had a picture of what the knife looked like, courtesy of the cooperative cutlery store owner. The prosecutors immediately secured a search warrant to again search O. J.'s house to look for this knife. When the police did not find it, they became convinced it was the murder weapon.

We, of course, asked our client whether he had purchased the knife; and when he admitted he did, we asked him what became of it. He said he put it on a shelf behind a mirror in his bedroom. I was immediately dispatched to O. J.'s home to see if it was still there. The mirror was flush with the wall, so unless you saw the hinges, you wouldn't know it opened up. I will never forget the moment I pulled the mirror open and saw the same knife I had seen on the front page of the *Enquirer*, sitting in an open box. My first thought was, "Oh shit, what do I do now?" The LAPD officers had missed it in their search. But if we could establish the knife was pristine, with no traces of blood or toolmarks, we could blow the prosecution out of the water when they claimed it was the murder weapon. We would only have to turn it over to the prosecution before trial if it turned out to be incriminating evidence. The worst thing I could do, however, was make myself a witness who would have to testify at the trial. I resisted the temptation to pick up the knife, closed the mirror, and went back to Bob Shapiro's office.

We decided to place our dilemma in the lap of the court. In a secret session, without the prosecutors present, we asked the court to appoint a special master to go to O. J.'s house, seize the knife, and keep it under seal while it was tested by forensic experts. The court agreed and appointed a retired judge to secretly retrieve the knife. To our immense relief, the tests revealed that the knife was as clean as the day it was purchased, except for the fingerprints of the judge who seized it. We didn't have to turn it over to the prosecution, so our little trap was sprung. After the prosecutors presented evidence that O. J. had purchased a knife and the knife was not found in a search of his home, we would call the retired judge to prove the knife was there all along and the forensic expert to prove the knife had not been used as a weapon. Although lawyers are required to provide discovery of the evidence they will present at trial, that obligation does not apply to rebuttal evidence. At least that's what we argued to Judge Ito. He made a very wise ruling that the rules of discovery should be implemented to prevent ambushes, not to facilitate them. The prosecution was informed of our discovery, and their claim that the stiletto knife was the murder weapon disappeared from the case.

Having been both a prosecutor and a defense lawyer, I was never troubled by the obligation to be a vigorous advocate on either side. I have always regarded the obligation of vigorous advocacy on both sides to be an essential prerequisite to the success of the adversary system. My greatest disappointments as a prosecutor were not the cases I lost, but the cases that were easier to win because the defense lawyer was unprepared or incompetent. For me, the case of *People v. O. J. Simpson* was a defense lawyer's dream because the resources were available to hire the best experts and investigators and pursue every avenue that might weaken the prosecution's case. Too often, our system denies to the indigent defendant the resources that are required to mount a vigorous defense. When we examine the hundreds of cases in which convicted defendants are exonerated by DNA testing that was not available at their trials, too often, part of the explanation was that they were deprived of a vigorous defense. Thus, even when a trial ends with a verdict in which the jury finds the requisite degree of certainty, we need to be open to the possibility that their conclusion was wrong. If they were wrong in acquitting the defendant, we just have to live with our mistake. The constitutional protection against double jeopardy absolutely precludes trying the defendant again. But if they were wrong in convicting the defendant, the conviction can be challenged. The development of DNA evidence has demonstrated that the number of times we were wrong and convicted someone who was innocent is much higher than we suspected. Barry Scheck and Peter Neufeld, my co-counsel during the O. J. trial, have devoted their careers to the national establishment of the Innocence Project, which was responsible for 303 DNA exonerations since 1989. In eighteen of the cases, the defendants were on death row awaiting execution.

All the factors identified as enhancing the risk of wrongful convictions (mistaken eyewitness identifications, false confessions, jail snitch testimony, and laboratory errors) are equally present in capital and noncapital cases and are just as prevalent in California as they are elsewhere in the country. These factors, of course, are also present in cases where there is no DNA evidence, like robberies and burglaries. The most disturbing statistic is that in 62 percent of the DNA exonerations, the defendant was black. Nearly all of them were indigent, although all of them were represented at their trial by lawyers. Thus, even when a defense lawyer is doing the job he or she is supposed to do, we may get a result that is not the truth. Guilty persons may go free. Innocent persons may be convicted. We do not have a perfect system. Should it be allowed to impose judgments of death, which cannot be corrected after they are carried out?

Some may find in these words confirmation of their deepest fears about our adversary system of justice. You might see what I write as another lawyer's game. I have perverted the concept of truth itself. Rather than objective conformity with reality, I have turned truth into the "prize" awarded to the winning player in a chess game. You may want to arraign me with all the lawyers condemned by Jonathan Swift for "proving by words multiplied for the purpose that white is black, and black is white according as they are paid."

I take the charge seriously and plead justification. With a clear conscience, I've spent most of my career as a teacher, training law students to realize that things are not always as they appear—that white may really be gray and that black may really be gray. But that is not to deny the existence of objective truth or to suggest that the pursuit of objective truth is not one of life's highest goals. My defense is that truth can only be defined in the context of its purpose. The purpose of a trial can best be served by an adversary system in which competing visions of the facts are contested. That contest must conform to rules that recognize that truth is not the only value we cherish. The acceptance of the ultimate resolution of the contest should only be measured by how vigorously we strived, not by whether we found the "truth." Nicholas Malebranche was a French philosopher who spent his whole life seeking a definition of truth, and forty years after Galileo's trial, he authored a two-volume work titled *Search after Truth. In Which Is Treated the Nature of the Human Mind and the Use That Must Be Made of It to Avoid Error in the Sciences.* Malebranche once imagined that he actually encountered God, who held in one hand truth and in the other the pursuit of truth, and asked him to choose. He said, "Lord, the truth is for thee alone; give me the pursuit." Thus, we might characterize our adversary system as giving neither side the truth, but only its pursuit. But the result of their contest should not be seen as a revelation of the truth or even as the end of the pursuit.

---

* First presented to the annual benefit dinner of Ponderosa High School, Shingle Springs, California, on March 22, 2013.

2

My Search for Utopia*

F OR FIVE HUNDRED years, the title of St. Thomas More's most famous work has been synonymous with the ideal of human perfection. Even Webster's dictionary now defines "utopia," with a small *u*, as "any place of ideal perfection" and a "utopian" as "one who believes in the perfectibility of human society; a visionary." I would now like to offer a public confession, which I hope will not startle you. I am a utopian. I firmly believe in the perfectibility of human society. I have spent a substantial part of my seventy-five years on this planet searching for utopia. In my wanderings, I have encountered many other utopians engaged in the same search.

I won't spend a lot of time analyzing St. Thomas More's book. It's amazing how many scholars have devoted serious efforts to that task and have come to opposite conclusions. C. S. Lewis said *Utopia* was a "jolly invention," intended as satire. The author of the *Chronicles of Narnia* concluded that readers whose interests are rigidly political do not understand *Utopia*, but everyone who has ever drawn an imaginary map responds at once. In response, UCLA professor Robert Adams wrote,

> C.S. Lewis always had some difficulty in seeing that people who weren't high Anglicans might yet have morals of a sort; thus he deprecated More the Communist as a means of enhancing More the Catholic martyr

Adams concludes that More meant *Utopia* with the same faculties of soul, and almost as seriously, as he meant his resistance to King Henry VIII. Putting *Utopia* into its historical context offers some useful insights.

Utopia was written in 1516. It was an era very much like our own. Europeans somehow sensed that they were standing at the threshold of a new world of discoveries that would test many of their assumptions about the world. Thomas More wrote all his observations of utopia as though they were coming from the mouth of a sea captain who had traveled to the new world with Amerigo Vespucci. Vespucci's accounts of his voyages were then much better known than those of Columbus. Indeed, the sea captain's description of his trip to utopia could easily place it in California.

Utopia was also written in an era of great religious upheaval. One year after its publication, Martin Luther nailed his ninety-five theses to the cathedral door in Wittenburg. Within a decade, the Reformation and the Counter-Reformation were wrenching realities throughout Europe. Thus, the description of a society that had achieved stability, justice, and prosperity found great popular success despite the fact that it was written in Latin by an Englishman.

The most important aspect in which Thomas More's world resembled our own, however, was the prevalence of human greed. The new world of discovery was viewed by many, first and foremost, as a new opportunity for exploitation and wealth. Even the Reformation was perceived by many as the opportunity to redistribute the vast wealth accumulated by the church to themselves. Consider this brief quotation from *Utopia* as if it was being spoken today:

> When I run over in my mind the various commonwealths flourishing today, so help me God, I can see nothing in them but a conspiracy of the rich, who are fattening up their own interests under the name and title of the commonwealth. They invent ways and means to hang onto whatever they have acquired by sharp practice, and then they scheme to oppress the poor by buying up their toil and labor as cheaply as possible. These devices become law as soon as the rich, speaking through the commonwealth, . . . say they must be observed.

These vehement words that Thomas More put in the mouth of his sea captain could have been lifted from St. Augustine's *The City of God*, written a thousand years before *Utopia*. They also echo the preaching of Girolamo Savonarola, the Dominican priest and reformer who was executed by burning in the Piazza della Signora only eighteen years before *Utopia* was published. They might also be heard today in the streets of London or New York or Cairo or Buenos Aires.

GERALD F. UELMEN

Utopia is, in its essence, a cry for justice. The search of today's utopians for the perfection of human society is based upon the conviction that human justice is achievable, not just a delusion. My search for utopia places me in distinguished company. My fellow utopians would include Mahatma Gandhi, Nelson Mandela, the Dalai Lama, and Pope Francis. My fellow utopians also include the worldwide order of Jesuits, celebrating their 475th birthday. In defining their mission, they have proclaimed that the promotion of justice is an absolute requirement for the service of faith. Their mission statement declares the following:

> There is a new challenge to our apostolic mission in a world increasingly interdependent but, for all that, divided by injustice: injustice not only personal but institutionalized: built into economic, social and political structures that dominate the life of nations and the international community.

True utopians are not daunted by the prospect of transforming the world. Like St. Thomas More, they believe humanity is fully capable of creating structures that serve the ends of justice. Are there any utopias in today's world that suggest the ideal is a real possibility?

My own search suggests there are many such places. Whatever one's religious faith, or lack thereof, one can find like-minded individuals who are devoting their lives to the pursuit of justice. My own Catholic faith led me to one such place, nestled in the hills of Tuscany, just south of Florence, the same Florence where Amerigo Vespucci was born nearly six hundred years ago. It's called Loppiano.

Loppiano is one manifestation of the vision of Chiara Lubich, a very remarkable woman who heard God's call in the midst of the bombing and destruction of Trent during World War II. As she and her companions watched their world and their dreams for the future collapse around them, they turned to the scriptures and rediscovered the foundations for a perfect and just human society in the words Christ spoke two thousand years ago: "Love one another as I have loved you" and "Wherever two or three are gathered in my name, I am with you, in your midst." They dedicated themselves to a new way of holy life, a fourth way—not the traditional life of matrimony, the classic style of religious community life, nor an individual consecration in the midst of the world. They introduced a new way of religious life into the Catholic church, and the church has embraced it. Their life is modeled on the life of a family—a family where reciprocal love is such that it generates the presence of Jesus in its midst. The uniqueness of this life is the constant striving for balance in holding together a lay foundation, an apostolic mission, a religious consecration, a daily family life, a profound sense of the church, a deep respect for the secular and religious culture of others, and an intense level of communication among all.

The movement is officially called the work of Mary because they imitate the mother of Jesus in the sense that their primary vocation is to understand and serve others and create the presence of Jesus in our midst. But the movement takes its popular name from the Italian word for "hearth," or family fireplace: the *focolare*. And the movement embraces all ways of life, including priests and nuns and married couples, as well as those who have chosen the single celibate life chosen by Chiara and her companions.

Our family met this movement in 1977 by attending a weeklong summer program called a Mariapolis. The Mariapolis is an astounding experience for a utopian. A community of mutual love emerges among three or four hundred people of incredibly diverse backgrounds and cultures. We learned some lasting lessons from that experience, lessons that we have gone back to reinforce many times since then: the discipline it takes to live in the present moment and not be fixated on our mistakes of the past or our dreams for the future, the transformation of our relationships with others when we actually see the presence of Christ within them, and for me, the hardest lesson of all, that the call to mutual love is not just a trumpet summoning me to a mountaintop, but a call to love those around me wherever I am, to love everyone, to be the first to love, and to love to the end.

As the Focolare movement has grown from a group of young girls in Trent to a worldwide movement with hundreds of centers in over fifty nations, a number of permanent Mariapolises have been built, small cities that bear witness to this life of unity and mutual love. Loppiano was the first. It has a thousand inhabitants. Many come from all parts of the world to spend two years of study and work in formation as *focolarini*, or the fire carriers. We first visited Loppiano with our children in 1978. After a three-day visit, our eleven-year-old daughter, Nancy, wrote home to her grandmother, "This is where I want to spend the rest of my life." She is there now, directing the women's musical group known as Gen Verde and presenting concert programs all over the world. Her younger sister, Amy, also joined the movement and is living in a Focolare house in Maryland while she teaches at Georgetown University Law Center. Their lives are truly an adventure in unity, and their success is evident in their joy and the harmony of their lives.

Many other little cities have now been established. Ottmaring in Germany was built by Catholics and Evangelicals as a sign of unity among diverse Christian denominations. Tagaytay in the Philippines is a meeting point for great religions of the East. O'Higgins in Chile and Vargum in Brazil both demonstrate a conquest over rigid differences between social classes. Fontem in the Cameroon is an adaptation of traditional African culture transformed by love. Montet in Switzerland closely resembles Loppiano. And finally, there's Mariapolis Luminosa near Hyde Park, New York. We have watched this American utopia grow from year to year for the past thirty years.

Many who have studied St. Thomas More's *Utopia* conclude his real source of inspiration was not a sea captain back from the new world, but the description of early Christian communities found in the Acts of the Apostles:

> And the multitudes of them that believed were of one heart and one soul; neither said any of them that any of the things that he possessed was his own; but they had all things in common. And with great power the apostles gave witness of the resurrection of the Lord Jesus; and great grace was upon them all.

From the example of these tiny early Christian communities, the entire world was transformed. As a utopian, I believe that can happen again in our own time. All it takes is love.

In our daily pursuit of justice, too often we find satisfaction in achieving the level of justice defined by the Romans: to give to each person what is rightfully his or hers. But the heart of the justice that we are called to is charity. Justice says "give to each person what is his or hers." Jesus said to "give to others even what is yours." Under our system of civil justice, one may legally die of hunger and neglect. Under the law of charity, no one can starve while any of us has bread. Justice is portrayed as a blind-folded goddess, with scales to carefully weigh her portions. Charity has eyes wide open to see the wretchedness of those in need, and she does not stop to weigh the gifts she offers.

Igino Giordani, an Italian scholar and statesman who was one of the earliest followers of Chiara Lubich in the Focolare movement, offered a beautiful reflection on the meaning of justice. He said,

> In a vivid figure of speech, Jesus calls justice a "hunger and a thirst." Blessed are they who hunger and thirst after justice: for they shall have their fill. Thus justice is to the Christian what food is to the hungry and drink to the thirsty. One who is hungry eats to the last crumb; one who is thirsty drinks to the last drop. . . . The desire for justice must be no less than a starving for it. And just as every day there is a need for food, so every day there is a need for justice. The beatitude implies that unhappiness resides not so much in the lack of justice as in the scant appetite men and women feel for it.

Thus, mutual love should define our appetite for justice. Chiara Lubich herself wrote,

> When we lovingly opened the Gospels or other books of the New Testament, during those long hours in the shelters, the passages that caught our attention were ones that spoke explicitly of love: "Only one thing is required. Love your neighbor as yourself." "Love your enemies." "Love one another." "Above all, let your love for one another be constant." These words seemed revolutionary to us, the key to a fullness of life we had not known before.

The revolutionary call to love, as the bond of perfection, is a call not to become holy individually, but in company with others. This brings me back to utopia. If we truly hunger and thirst for justice, we are all utopians. The gospel of Jesus Christ calls all of us to be utopians. Radical? Revolutionary? The ideal of the human perfection we seek does require a radical transformation and a revolutionary movement. It's as radical and revolutionary as the New Testament itself. It requires that we love one another.

---

*   From an address to the St. Thomas More Society of Santa Clara County, California, March 2000.

3

What Matters Most to Me*

WHAT MATTERS MOST to me is having a vision, a goal, an ideal. The mountaintop. What drives me. It's an ideal I sometimes think I can never completely achieve. Yet I know it is achievable because I catch glimpses of others who seem to be there or at least are close to the mountaintop. How did they get there? Can I get there through the same route? Or do I have to find my own way?

There are times in my life when I feel as though I am traveling on the day train. I can look out the window and see the mountaintop. I can see the streams of others struggling to reach the peak. But more often, I find myself on the night train. I'm still moving, often at a high rate of speed. But I can't see where I'm going. I know the mountain is still out there, but I can't see it. And I can't see anyone else climbing it. There have been times in my life when I thought I had arrived. I stood on a high peak and thought to myself, "I've made it. I've arrived." Then disillusionment sets in. I've fooled myself. This isn't the mountaintop of my vision. I still have further to climb. I stop to rest, but I know my rest is only a temporary respite.

I cannot honestly say that I think of my vision, my ideal, my mountaintop as God or Jesus Christ, although I am a believer. My faith tells me that God is love, but I don't think you need to believe in God to believe in the power of love. I would rather describe my ideal as perfect love or perfect truth or perfect justice. I'll try to explain what I mean by these terms, but I think truth and justice are ultimately manifestations of love. It may seem strange to see a lawyer equate love with truth and justice, but I have long since concluded that the pursuit of truth and the pursuit of justice demand the pursuit of love. You cannot pursue the truth until you are ready to love, and you cannot pursue justice in the absence of love. And the glimpses I see of perfect love in the world may well be glimpses of God.

What do I mean by the pursuit of "perfect" love? So often in my life, when I question my motives, I discover that even though I'm reaching out to others and helping them climb *their* mountains, I'm doing it with the expectation of some reward or recognition. Or I'm doing it because I deem the recipients as deserving. I have judged them to be "worthy" of my love. The ideal of perfect love is an aspiration I can rarely achieve, where I am willing to give my life totally and completely to another with no conditions or expectations. Yet I know it is possible because I have seen it manifested in my life.

The first example I find of the pursuit of perfect love manifested in my life is the example of my godfather Robert Nystrom. When Bob stood at the baptismal font where I was baptized as an infant in Greendale, Wisconsin, seventy-five years ago and renounced Satan on my behalf, he had a lot going for him. He was a stellar law student at Marquette University. He was popular and well-liked. As a high school senior, he won a trip to the 1939 World's Fair in New York in a contest in which everyone in town voted for the students to be sent. After completing his first year of law school and becoming engaged to the love of his life (a young nurse in Milwaukee), Bob enlisted in the U.S. Army Air Forces. After his training, he was sent to England to serve as navigator aboard the B-24s that were flying bombing missions over enemy territory. The young men who flew those planes knew they were putting their lives on the line every time they taxied down the runway. More than half of them didn't come back. Bob flew two missions. They believe his plane went down over the English Channel. The remains of Bob and his crew were never found. When his personal effects were sent to his parents, they included a small wallet of photos, with a photo of me at the age of three. As a kid, I was often privileged to spend school vacations with Bob's parents, my uncle Charlie and aunt Mary. Even as a child, I could sense the emptiness that losing their only child stamped upon their lives. I've often reflected that I was privileged to live the life that Bob was ready to sacrifice—that he really gave his life for me. I was privileged to finish law school and marry the nurse I fell in love with. I was privileged to have the children he never had and pursue the legal career he would never know.

On a trip to England, my wife and I travelled to Norfolk to find Seething Airfield from which Bob flew his missions. It is still there, and the control tower has been made into a tiny museum. I was impressed by how many still remembered. I only knew Bob through the cousins he loved, including my dad. They are all gone now, but the love remains.

Another manifestation of the pursuit of perfect love in my life was the example of my sister Jean. Jean was born in 1947, when I was six years old. She was the eighth and final child born to my parents. She was born with the same congenital disease that took the lives of two of my siblings. A progressive atrophy of the muscles first crippled them, and when they died at the age of three and four, they could no longer hold up their heads. The doctors told my parents that the same fate awaited Jean, but my father rejected their verdict. Each night before we went to bed, he gathered the family in Jean's bedroom to pray. I still remember the prayer we would say together: "Jesus, bless Mommy and Daddy, Tommy and Donny, Jerry and Cookie, and Johnny and Jeanie." Then we would pray "To Mother Cabrini for Jeannie" and say a Hail Mary. Jean turned out to be one of Mother Cabrini's miracles. The progress of her muscular atrophy was arrested, and Jean lived to the age of fifty-eight. Although she was a quadriplegic and spent her entire life in a wheelchair, she was the strongest person I have ever known. Even though she depended on others for her physical needs, she took charge of her life and filled it with acts of love for others. She pursued an education, earning a PhD. She pursued two careers, first as a speech therapist, then as a psychologist. Then to our utter amazement, she pursued a pregnancy and gave birth to a child. It could have killed her, and almost did, but when I stood at the baptismal font as Julia's godfather and renounced Satan on her behalf, I knew I was holding another manifestation of perfect love. For the last fifteen years of her life, Jean lived in Guatemala. Much of her declining energy was devoted to the building of a library for the children of the village of Dueñas. It's called Open Windows. She believed that by offering these children books to read, a place to study, and computers to play with, they could open a window to the world beyond their tiny village. We're hoping to keep that dream alive. The love remains.

One of the most significant manifestations of the pursuit of perfect love in my life has been the inspiration of Chiara Lubich, the woman who founded the Focolare movement, described above. The Focolare movement was born in the bomb shelters of Trent while B-24s were dropping bombs on the city. When I try to sort out this irony, of a loving man dropping bombs and a loving woman building a community of love and unity out of the rubble, I begin to understand what it means to say that God is love.

The ideal of perfect love is not easy to pursue. I think it's especially hard in the profession I have chosen and which my wife eventually chose as well. It's a profession that thrives on conflict and the model we choose when conflicts cannot otherwise be resolved to replicate the conflict in a courtroom, with the lawyers called upon to serve as adversaries. I truly enjoy the strategizing and gamesmanship that goes on during a trial and eagerly do everything the law allows to advance my client's position and undercut the position of the opposition. But how can this be reconciled with pursuing the ideal of perfect love?

If the ideal of perfect love requires us to love our enemies and pray for those who persecute us, every trial presents a challenging opportunity. Loving your opponent does not mean surrendering to him or her and letting him or her win. But it does mean respecting his or her humanity. Dehumanizing your adversaries is always the first step to successful warfare. Unfortunately, too many lawyers regard it as the first step to successful trial strategy.

I must confess that I have occasionally encountered clients, opposing lawyers, and even judges who were hard to love; and I often fell short of my ideal. Trial adversaries often regard your efforts to love them as a sign of weakness to be exploited. I must further confess that I take special pleasure in defeating such adversaries and showing them that willingness to love is a sign of strength, not weakness.

If everyone was pursuing perfect love with equal vigor, we might have some hope of achieving perfect truth or perfect justice. But our inability to achieve perfect truth or perfect justice should not dissuade us from the pursuit of both. In the Gospel of St. Matthew, chapter 5, Jesus delivers his Sermon on the Mount. In it, he concludes,

> You have heard that it was said, "you shall love your neighbor and hate your enemy." But I say to you, love your enemies and pray for those who persecute you, that you may be children of your heavenly father. For he makes his sun rise on the bad and the good, and causes rain to fall on the just and the unjust. For if you love those who love you, what recompense will you have? Do not the tax collectors do the same? And if you greet your brothers only, what is unusual

about that? Do not the pagans do the same? *So be perfect, just as your heavenly Father is perfect.*

This passage is one of only two places in the Gospels where the word "perfect" is used. And in both cases, the perfection referred to is the perfection of love and its pursuit.

---

* From a lecture series sponsored by the Ignatian Center for Jesuit Education at Santa Clara University, April 2008.

4

Sun Prairie (A Poem)

M Y FATHER, FRANCIS T. Uelmen, passed away on May 12, 2003. My mother, Trudy, put his cremains on a shelf in her closet and instructed us to wait until she died so their remains could be interred together. After Mom died in August of 2011, the entire family traveled back to Sun Prairie, Wisconsin the town where my mother was raised, to deposit the ashes of both my parents, as well as some ashes of my sister Jean, at Sacred Heart Cemetery, where two of their children had been laid to rest. To mark the occasion, I wrote the following poem:

Burying what remains of Mom and Dad and Jean,
beneath Wisconsin sod at a time when it's green,
takes me back to the day when I came to this same place
with my brother Dale in a box.
He was four, and I was seven.
They told me he had gone to heaven.
I asked, "Why him and not me instead?"
I could not understand why he was dead.
"God has a plan," they said. "Someday you will see."
Now I have lived the life he never had,
still searching for the plan God has for me.
It brought me once again to this same place,
asking the same questions and hearing the same answers.
But I am not alone. Gathered here with me
are those whom I love, my family—
except for Mom and Dad and Jean and Janice and Dale and Tom
and Mary Lee.
And now I understand that God's plan has no end.

III

A System of Justice

1

Three Cheers or Two Tiers?*

I VIVIDLY REMEMBER the first time I saw *2001: A Space Odyssey* in 1968. The "new millennium" seemed so far away it was easy to believe we'd all be zipping around from one space station to another when it arrived. Now that the new millennium has arrived, I must confess my disappointment. We are still riding buses, and we're still stuck in traffic jams; and while my students have greater access to information, they just don't seem to be any smarter than those I taught thirty years ago. Yet *2001* is still a marvelous metaphor for our struggle to control technology. The astronaut's frantic effort to turn off the computer is replicated thousands of times a day as we struggle with our addiction to instant gratification of every curiosity. I'm still amazed at how many Americans have not discovered that the little red button on their remote empowers them to turn off their television sets whenever they choose.

While I'm not a full-fledged Luddite, I am skeptical of those who predict a rosy future for our courts. In 1994, then chief justice Malcolm Lucas (of the California Supreme Court) convened a blue-ribbon study of our court system to set the agenda for "2020." The Commission on the Future of the Courts envisioned a future populated with really smart judges and really cooperative lawyers, a world in which the legislature had apparently been suspended and the initiative process abolished. Hope overcame experience. In short, 2020 was portrayed as a mythical paradise in which litigation was declining because the law had been "settled" and litigants had less to fight about.

My vision of where we're headed is more pessimistic. Progress gives us more to fight about, not less. And does anyone actually believe human greed is decreasing? I believe that the competition among lawyers will intensify, the bar will divide between two hemispheres with an ocean between, the quality of our judges will decline, and the level of public satisfaction with the public justice system will keep shrinking. Those who can afford it will still travel first-class with a private system of justice eager to serve them. Those who can't will be left behind. The only question is how far behind.

The Public School Analogy

There's a depressing analogy for the likely future of the California court system. It's the California public school system. In the course of the past thirty years, we've watched California's public school system sink in a morass of neglect, confusion, and incompetence. It went from one of the best in the country to one of the worst. Low test scores, teacher shortages, lack of books and computers, and overcrowded, shabby classrooms confirm the decline.

What happened? While there's plenty of blame to go around, the bottom line is simply that our priorities got rearranged. The competition for our tax dollars became too intense, and the schools were elbowed out. When the public pie is carved, the number of elbows is determinative. The size of any system's slice will depend upon the political clout of the "stakeholders," those who perceive they have something to gain or lose from the size of the slice. Thirty years ago, those who had a "stake" in California's public schools included a substantial majority of the electorate. Roughly 90 percent of parents were sending their kids to public schools, and employers saw the public schools as the source for their future workforce.

Today, one out of four children is attending private schools, being schooled at home, or being bused to alternative "charter" schools. This brain drain feeds a downward spiral because the parents who opt out are frequently the parents who are most involved in their children's education. Studies consistently confirm that the best student performers are those whose parents are involved. The public schools are then left with the dregs—a disproportionate supply of students who don't want to learn, who have serious learning disabilities, or whose parents can't or won't get involved. Disheartened teachers often leave for lower-paying jobs in the private sector where at least they can teach responsive, motivated students.

It's not likely that a huge infusion of cash to reduce class sizes in California's public schools will fix the problem. Reducing class size means supplying a lot more teachers and classrooms. Our best and brightest college graduates are not flocking to meet this new demand, and taxpayer support for new classroom construction is lagging. If the initial investment doesn't produce dramatic results, the political clout needed to sustain this effort will dissipate. The underlying problem is that not enough Californians feel they have a stake in the system anymore. The fastest-growing sector of the electorate—those who vote—are our senior citizens. Their kids are through school, and now they are more concerned with health care issues and public safety. The immigrant minorities who fuel the largest influx into our public school system exercise little political clout.

Ironically, at a moment in our history when new technology and the information age define our future, the gap between those who can afford private education and those whose only choice is public education may measure the chasm between the haves and the have-nots. The chasm is growing deeper and wider every day.

A Two-Tiered Justice System

In all likelihood, the California court system will reflect this dichotomy. Two "systems" of justice will coexist: (1) a private system, where the judges are well-paid achievers, the conference rooms are clean and comfortable, the technology works, and justice is dispensed with speed and efficiency; and (2) a public system, where underpaid bureaucrats serve as the judges, and long lines of litigants wait in run-down courthouses with peeling paint on the walls.

To put it bluntly, many "stakeholders" are leaving the public justice system. Who can blame them? Private dispute resolution offers many advantages. You can pick your judge. You're not stuck with a tyrant whose greatest concern seems to be getting through the crowded calendar by noon and shuffling off the "problems" to someone else. You can resolve your case in complete privacy, excluding curiosity seekers and inquisitive news reporters. You can set hearings for times that accommodate everyone's schedule in pleasant modern surroundings. It might even be cheaper. At the rate you're paying your lawyers, any savings in time actually reduces your litigation costs.

As those who can afford it opt into the private justice system, the public system is left with a disproportionate share of the dregs just as the public school system is—the lawyers and litigants who want to crush each other and play hardball, the growing legions of *pro per* litigants who can't afford to hire a lawyer at all, and, of course, those accused of crimes who have no choice. Judges who began their careers full of zeal are burning out at an alarming rate. There is little relief from the steady flow of the most demanding cases, the most obnoxious litigants, and the least prepared lawyers. Many are retiring at the earliest opportunity. It's not primarily greed that drives them away, although many will earn three times what they earned as public judges. The real attraction is the opportunity to control their own workflow spigot and to regain their equilibrium. The boosters of private judging say, "You should be grateful to us. We're relieving the pressure on the system by removing the more complex disputes." True, but they are also removing the incentive for their well-heeled clients to support the public justice system, and they are enticing the best judges to leave for greener pastures.

Ironically, our public justice system is finding it difficult not only to retain experienced judges but also to maintain the flow of jurors so essential to preserving the right to jury trial. In some areas, less than one-tenth of those summoned as jurors even bother to return the questionnaire.

A little more money could go a long way toward solving some of these problems: Raise the salaries and improve the retirement benefits for judges, fund a system of judicial sabbaticals to alleviate burnout, increase the *per diem* paid to jurors, and provide comfortable waiting rooms. While the chief justice might have all these on her list, she's discovering they don't rank very high on the priority list of the governor or the legislature. Is this because the "stakeholders" in the system of public justice no longer wield much clout? When she gets in line for the judicial slice of the pie, can you guess who's moved ahead in front of her? The public schools!

Lawyers as Stakeholders

One might expect that California lawyers could do a lot to turn this situation around. If any group is a major "stakeholder" in our system of public justice, it's the lawyers. And when it comes to political clout, lawyers have some of the biggest elbows around.

That's all changed too. Lots of lawyers have political clout, but they don't flex their muscles for the public justice system. Their political agendas have become much more parochial. The plaintiff's bar expends its energy and resources battling initiatives proposed by the insurance bar. The corporate bar is more concerned with the private justice system than the public one. When they go to court, they prefer to be in federal court. They're already paying for *their* judges—why pay twice? They may even learn a few new tricks from the battle over public school funding and start demanding vouchers to pay for private judges.

The California State Bar has been defanged. There are even those who insist that the state bar's lobbying for more judges or higher judicial salaries or increased juror *per diem* is an unlawful expenditure of state bar funds for political purposes.

The sad reality is that the bar is also divided by the same chasm that divides the rest of our society. The lawyers who serve clients who can afford the private system of justice are not the same lawyers who answer the calendar calls in our public courts. As demonstrated in the study of *Chicago Lawyers*, there are really *two* bars, and they don't have much to do with each other. The bar that serves corporate clients is getting richer, and the bar that competes for individual clients is getting poorer. The competition for clients among lawyers who serve the public has become more intense, and a substantial part of their income may depend upon court-appointed cases and court-determined rates. The agenda for increasing those rates has fallen victim to the same lack of clout as the rest of the public justice system's agenda.

Among the greatest ironies of the last century is that we quintupled the supply of lawyers yet left the legal needs of the poor largely unmet. Funding for legal services programs and indigent defense services is declining, while the need is increasing. This adds to the burdens imposed on the courts. When the poor and disenfranchised come seeking justice without the aid of a lawyer, judges and court personnel must assume new roles as teachers and facilitators.

Judges as Bureaucrats

The past century has also witnessed radical transformation of the judicial office and those who are filling judicial vacancies. Judges used to assume the bench after a successful career in private practice, and many brought with them a broad base of experience as litigators. With the increased specialization and bifurcation of the bar, those with substantial civil litigation experience become a rarer commodity as judicial candidates. The politicization of criminal justice issues turned the district attorneys' offices into the chief source of judicial candidates. Those who do come from the private bar more often come from the bar that serves individual clients rather than from the large firms serving corporate clients.

One reason corporate clients prefer the private justice system is that they are more likely to find a judge who really understands their problems. The public justice system may have a handful of judges who came from the hemisphere of the bar that serves corporate clients, but it just doesn't seem to do a good job of matching judges with their real talents. Judicial assignments are generally made by seniority. If you are starting a judicial career late after years as a high-power litigator, a judicial appointment may be a ticket to terminal boredom, shuffling through crowded calendars of small claims, *pro per* divorces, or traffic cases.

Compounding the problem is the sinking level of judicial salaries. Today, even deputy district attorneys are taking a pay cut when they accept judicial appointments. While the admirable goal of serving the public still motivates most judicial aspirants, they soon learn that the public is not a very appreciative employer. They become part of a grinding bureaucracy in which the best strategy for survival is to keep your head down. The judges who make waves are most likely to be targeted for an election challenge.

Searching for Solutions

The forces that are pushing our court system into a two-tier model are forces largely beyond our control. Every aspect of our lives in the twenty-first century will be lived on two tiers: health care, housing, transportation, and education. The rich will get richer and live very comfortable lives. Those who are not will strive to become rich, but most won't make it and lead lives of quiet desperation. Why should we anticipate that our court system will be able to straddle the chasm?

Returning to our public school system, however, we might find some strategies worth emulating. Those who are committed to the excellence of public education—and there are still many—have realized that public schools must still compete for students. The best way to compete is to offer choices. It can no longer be a "one size fits all" enterprise. High achievers should be identified and given the challenges that will keep them engaged. Those with learning disabilities must also be identified and provided an environment in which they too can thrive. That still takes more resources, so the creative alternatives have to be aggressively marketed and sold to the public. Visibility of what the public schools are doing and explanations of why they are doing it have become the key to public support.

Voter education and mobilization are also key elements to turning around the fate of public schools. Being a "stakeholder" needs to be transformed into a communitarian concept. We all have a stake in our public schools, whether our kids attend them or not, because they shape the quality of our community life. The schools need to become visible community centers, not isolated bastions.

Can our public courts learn something from the example of our public schools? The future will arrive, whether we make the effort or not. But our efforts may have a lot to do with the kind of future we face. The breadth of the gap between our two tiers will measure our failure.

---

*   From *California Litigation*, vol. 13, no. 1, p. 4 (2000).

2

The Six Major Causes of Wrongful Convictions

F ROM 2004 TO 2008, I served as executive director of the California Commission on the Fair Administration of Justice, created by the California State Legislature to investigate the causes of the conviction of innocent persons and make recommendations to minimize the danger of wrongful conviction. In the final report that I authored, six major causes of wrongful convictions were identified.

1. Mistaken Eyewitness Identifications

A comprehensive compilation of all exonerations in the United States from 1989 through 2003 was published by a group of researchers at the University of Michigan led by Professor Samuel R. Gross. The researchers confined their study to cases in which there was an official act declaring a defendant not guilty of a crime for which he or she had previously been convicted (such as a pardon based upon evidence of innocence) or a dismissal after new evidence of innocence emerged (such as DNA testing). They identified 340 such cases, twenty-seven of which occurred in the State of California. Of the 340 cases, 60 percent had been convicted of murder, and 36 percent had been convicted of rape or sexual assault. They note two possible explanations for the high prevalence of murder cases: false convictions are more likely to be discovered in murder and death penalty cases because of the intensive level of postconviction review given to these cases, or false convictions are more likely to *occur* in murder and death penalty cases because of enhanced police and prosecutorial zeal. There may be other explanations. We do not know whether wrongful convictions are much more common than realized throughout the system.

One explanation for the high prevalence of rape and sexual assault cases among exonerations is recent improvements in DNA technology that can now be used not only to identify a perpetrator of rape at trial, but also to clear an individual of the crime both before and after conviction. Mistaken eyewitness identification was involved in 88 percent of the rape and sexual assault cases. This suggests that unexposed mistaken identification could be present in other convictions that heavily rely upon eyewitness identifications, such as robbery cases, where DNA evidence is not normally present. Among the eighty cases in which rape defendants were subsequently exonerated and the race of both parties was known, thirty-nine of the cases involved black men who were wrongfully convicted of raping white women, and nearly all these cases involved mistaken eyewitness identifications. Since less than 10 percent of all rapes in the United States involve white victims and black perpetrators, the fact that a disproportionate number of the rape exonerations involve white victims misidentifying black suspects suggests that the risk of error is greater in cross-racial identifications. Cross-racial identifications are more common in robbery cases than in rape cases. Research has consistently confirmed that cross-racial identifications are not as reliable as within-race identifications.

2. False Confessions

False confessions were identified as the second most frequent cause of wrongful convictions in the University of Michigan study. Although it may seem surprising that factually innocent persons would falsely confess to the commission of serious crimes, research provides ample evidence that this phenomenon occurs with greater frequency than widely assumed. Professors Steven Drizin and Richard A. Leo identify 125 cases that occurred between 1972 and 2002, with 31 percent of them occurring in the five years up to 2003. Eight of these examples, or 6 percent of the sample, occurred in California cases. The overwhelming majority of the false confession cases identified by Drizin and Leo occurred in very serious cases: 81 percent were homicide cases, followed by 9 percent rape cases. Not all false confessions lead to conviction. Of the eight California cases identified by Drizin and Leo, none of the defendants charged was convicted of the crimes to which they falsely confessed. It should be noted, of course, that even where charges do not result in conviction, the pendency of charges based upon false confessions can impose tremendous burdens upon the accused and their families, as well as the victims and their families. The accused is often in custody for months prior to being released. The research suggests that false confessions are often extracted from the most vulnerable suspects. One-third (33 percent) of the Drizin and Leo sample were juveniles, another 22 percent were mentally disabled, and at least 10 percent were mentally ill. But even fully competent and rational persons may be victimized by coercive interrogation techniques.

3.   Testimony by Jailhouse Snitches

The motivation for jail snitches to testify against a fellow prisoner is frequently the expectation of some reward in the form of reduction of charges, eligibility for bail, leniency in sentencing, or better conditions of confinement. In a report by the Northwestern University School of Law's Center on Wrongful Convictions, the use of such informants was identified among the three most prevalent factors in the wrongful convictions of death row inmates. After a review of the cases of 111 persons released from the nation's death rows after they were exonerated, from 1973 through 2004, the center found use of false testimony from informants in 45.9 percent of the cases. That made false informant testimony the *leading* cause of wrongful convictions in U.S. *capital* cases, followed by erroneous eyewitness identifications (25.2 percent of the cases) and false confessions (14.4 percent of the cases). While none of the 111 cases in the Center on Wrongful Convictions report took place in California, the frequent use of informant testimony in capital cases appears in California capital cases as well. Michael Laurence, the director of the California Habeas Corpus Resource Center, explained the reasons for the high prevalence of the use of arrested or charged informants in capital cases. In his opinion, while they are rarely needed to supply evidence of the defendant's guilt of the underlying crime, they often provide crucial testimony to prove the alleged special circumstances that make the defendant eligible for the death penalty or to provide evidence of lack of remorse to persuade the jury to select death as the appropriate penalty. State public defender Michael Hersek reported that of the 117 death penalty appeals currently pending in his office, seventeen featured testimony by in-custody informants, and another six included testimony by informants who were in constructive custody. Thus, confidence in the reliability of the testimony of arrested or charged informant witnesses is a matter of continuing concern to ensure that the administration of justice in California is just, fair, and accurate.

4. Inaccurate Forensic Science Evidence

The presentation of forensic science evidence is often the turning point in a criminal trial. Today, the news carries reports of erroneous forensic identifications of hair, bullets, handwriting, footprints, bite marks, and even venerated fingerprints. The Innocence Project at Cardozo School of Law identified forensic science testing errors in 63 percent of eighty-six DNA exoneration cases analyzed, the second most common factor contributing to wrongful convictions in that study.

As recently noted in the report of the Ad Hoc Innocence Committee of the American Bar Association, three developments in the 1990s dramatically altered the judicial approach to scientific evidence. First, unlike any other forensic discipline that preceded it, DNA profiling entered the courts only after it had been extensively validated through broad research and elaborate quality assurance programs that included rigorous proficiency testing, standards for declaring a match, and the appropriate content of a report. This set a "gold standard" against which other forensic sciences are now measured and often found wanting. Raising the standards of the other forensic disciplines is all the more critical since it is the non-DNA disciplines that comprise the bulk of a crime lab's output. DNA testing constitutes approximately 5 percent of the work of crime labs. Second, the decision of the U.S. Supreme Court in *Daubert v. Merrell Dow Pharm., Inc.*, 509 U.S. 579 (1993), established a more rigorous standard of admissibility for expert testimony, requiring it to be based upon sufficient facts or data, the product of reliable principles and methods, and reliably applied to the facts of the case.

The third development was the exposure of serious abuse even in DNA testing in a number of crime labs throughout the United States. Serious misconduct of forensic experts led to the reexamination of many cases in West Virginia, Oklahoma, Montana, and Texas. The Houston Police Department shut down the DNA and serology section of its crime laboratory in early 2003 after a television exposé revealed serious deficiencies in the lab's procedures. Two men who were falsely incriminated by botched lab work were released after subsequent DNA testing proved their innocence. In Virginia, an independent lab confirmed that DNA tests conducted by the state lab were botched and misinterpreted in the case of a man who came within days of being executed. The governor ordered a broader investigation of the state lab to determine whether these problems were endemic. California has occasionally endured laboratory scandals. In 1994, more than one thousand felony convictions were jeopardized by the revelation that a San Francisco police lab technician had been certifying that samples contained illicit narcotics without performing laboratory tests.

5. Incompetence of Defense Lawyers

Many of the causes of wrongful convictions that the commission recognized (mistaken eyewitness identifications, false confessions, perjured jail informant testimony, faulty forensic evidence) could have been exposed and addressed if the defendant had been represented by competent, zealous counsel who had fully investigated and prepared the case. A study of the first seventy-four DNA exonerations in the United States found that defense lawyer incompetence was a factor in 32 percent of the cases.

In California, the primary responsibility for providing competent counsel at the trial level to indigent accused falls upon each individual county. California's fifty-eight counties meet this obligation in a variety of ways. Thirty-three counties (57 percent) have created one or more institutional public defender offices as county departments to serve as the primary provider of criminal defense services to indigent accused. This includes every county in California with a population in excess of five hundred thousand, with the exception of San Mateo County. Contract defenders are the primary provider of indigent felony and misdemeanor representation in twenty-four counties (41 percent). Eight counties have contracted with a single law firm, which provides various types of representation through branch offices. Some counties contract with solo practitioners. Several counties, for example, have four different solo contract defenders handling different portions of the caseload; and one county has seven separate contract defenders. The amount of compensation afforded by these contracts is often based upon a fixed fee per case or a flat fee for the expected annual caseload. While this type of system is heavily concentrated in rural counties having populations of less than one hundred thousand, it also exists in some urban counties in which public defenders are the primary providers. Many counties with a public defender office, for example, use a contract defender to handle cases in which the public defender declares unavailability due to conflicts or overload.

In April, 2000, the U.S. Department of Justice funded a national study of contracting for indigent defense services. The study report began with an example of how critics' worst fears about indigent defense contract systems came true. The example came from Shasta County in California. It is a very sobering account:

> In 1997 and 1998, a Shasta county agreed to pay a low-bid contractor slightly more than $400,000 a year to represent half of the county's indigent defendants. The contractor was a private practitioner who employed two associates and two secretaries, but no paralegal or investigator. The contract required the contractor to handle more than 5,000 cases each year. All of the contractor's expenses came out of the contract. To make a profit, the contractor had to spend as little time as possible on each case. In 1998, the contractor took fewer than 20 cases—less than 0.5 percent of the combined felony and misdemeanor caseload—to trial. One of the contractor's associates was assigned only cases involving misdemeanors. She carried a caseload of between 250 and 300 cases per month. The associate had never tried a case before a jury. She was expected to plead cases at the defendant's first appearance in court so she could move on to the next case. One afternoon, however, the associate was given a felony case scheduled for trial the following week. The case involved multiple felony and misdemeanor charges. When she looked at the case file, the associate discovered that no pretrial motions had been filed, no witness list had been compiled, no expert witnesses had been endorsed, and no one had been subpoenaed. In short, there had been no investigation of any kind into the case, and she had no one to help her with the basics of her first jury trial. The only material in the case file was five pages of police reports. In these reports, she found evidence of a warrantless search, which indicated strong grounds for suppression. She told the judge she was not ready to proceed and that a continuance was necessary to preserve the defendant's sixth amendment right to counsel. The continuance was denied. The associate refused to move forward with the case. The contractor's

other associate took over the case and pled the client guilty to all charges. The associate who had asked for a continuance was fired.

Flat-fee contracts create an unethical conflict of interest for defense lawyers. The more they spend on investigation and expert witnesses, the less compensation they take home. The costs of investigation and experts should be separately reimbursed.

6. Misconduct by Prosecutors

Professor Cookie Ridolfi of Santa Clara University School of Law located 2,130 California cases in the previous ten years in which claims of prosecutorial misconduct were raised. Courts concluded that prosecutorial misconduct did occur in 443 of these cases, or 21 percent. In 390 of these 443 cases, however, the court concluded the misconduct was harmless error and affirmed the conviction. In fifty-three cases, the misconduct resulted in a reversal of the conviction. The most common forms of misconduct found were failing to disclose exculpatory evidence and improper argument.

Pursuant to the California Business and Professions Code, there should have been a report made to the state bar in each of the fifty-three cases in which prosecutorial misconduct resulted in a reversal. In a follow-up to Professor Ridolfi's research, chief trial counsel Scott Drexel of the state bar testified that after checking half of these fifty-three cases to determine whether any of them resulted in a report to the state bar, he had yet to find a single example of a report by a court of misconduct resulting in reversal of a conviction. This suggests that California judges are simply ignoring their statutory duty to report prosecutorial misconduct to the state bar for possible disciplinary action.

3

Victims' Rights*

IN JUNE 1982, California voters approved an initiative measure to modify evidentiary exclusionary rules, enhance sentences, reformulate the insanity defense, and make numerous changes in the admissibility of evidence in criminal trials. The initiative measure was titled the Victims' Bill of Rights but is more widely known as Proposition 8. Eight years later, another initiative measure was adopted, which made even more extensive changes in the procedure governing criminal trials. It was titled the Crime Victims Justice Reform Act and is generally known as Proposition 115. I was a very vocal opponent of both Proposition 8 and Proposition 115 and believe both of these initiatives accomplished more harm than good. My opposition was not based on any philosophical objection against granting greater rights to victims of crime. I thought, for example, that giving victims the right to be heard at time of sentencing was a positive improvement, and I believe our experience confirms that. My real opposition was based on a commitment to "truth in labeling." I thought both propositions were rather cynical efforts to capture public support for radical changes in the criminal justice system—by labeling them "victims' rights" measures when their real purpose was to shift greater power into the hands of prosecutors while offering very little in terms of real relief for victims of crime.

While I recognized the need for reform of the criminal justice system, I thought that meaningful reform required a broader base than a back-room closet of the District Attorneys Association. We are now at a critical juncture in California, calling for some realistic reassessment of where the victims' rights movement has brought us. My candid assessment is that it has simply brought us to the point of bankruptcy: intellectual bankruptcy, by disguising criminal justice system complexity behind simplistic labels that actually impede us in our quest for justice; fiscal bankruptcy, by diverting resources that are badly needed for education and social programs into a bottomless pit of prison expansion; and moral bankruptcy, by creating a political climate where real reform is impossible because political leaders are obsessed with the fear that any rational consideration of alternatives will result in their being labeled "soft on crime."

First, let me address the intellectual bankruptcy of the use of labels. Labels powerfully influence our criminal justice system. I first learned this lesson as a young prosecutor assigned to the "organized crime" division of the U.S. Attorney's Office. I remember how impressive it was to see the transformation in everyone's treatment of a case once it was labeled an "organized crime" case. A simple bookmaking case could be transformed into a cause célèbre with a visible, measurable impact upon judge, jury, and the media. We even acquired a huge rubber stamp so our files could be marked "Organized Crime Division." We always carried the files so that the rubber-stamped label was clearly visible when we marched into court. We knew the power of a label. For a moment, just reflect on what kinds of images the label "victim" conjures up in your mind. Our immediate reaction to the word "victim" is compassionate concern for the helpless innocent and anger directed against the guilty victimizer, the "criminal." At its best, our criminal justice system should permit us to transcend these labels and sort out the complexities of human frailty. Anyone who has participated in this process should appreciate how difficult it frequently is to clearly separate victims from victimizers. Who is the "victim," for example, when a battered wife finally summons the courage to strike back at her tormentor while his back is turned? Who were the "victims" in the McMartin "child abuse" fiasco? When we allow labels to serve as the measure of our compassion, we disguise this complexity. For me, the dark side of the victims' rights movement is its insistence that compassion be reserved to those we label "victims" and denied to those we label "criminals." Our prisons are also full of victims. Many inmates were victims of abuse as children. Most of them are victims of the disease of addiction to alcohol or drugs. I realize such diseases do not rank very high on our compassion index, but I would suggest this may have more to do with our own ignorance about their etiology than the moral failings of their victims. The banner of the victims' rights movement declares, however, that the purpose of sentencing is punishment. We have transformed our correctional system into a complex of human warehouses. Over the entrance, we have declared, "Abandon any hope or pretense of rehabilitation, ye who enter here."

In 1992, the California legislature enacted a measure to permit the early release of prisoners who were terminally ill and allow them to return to their families during the final stages of their fatal disease. The measure was vetoed by the governor. Apparently, enactment would have encroached on our strict reservation of compassion only for those who have been labeled "victims." Those who have been labeled "criminals" presumably deserve no compassion, even when they are dying of AIDS. The cruelest manifestation of this labeling phenomenon is the transformation of the debate over capital punishment into a debate over victims' rights. The suggestion is heard with increasing frequency that the real reason we should execute criminals instead of confining them for life without possibility of parole is to provide solace and comfort to the families of their victims. I would not expect any family member of a murder victim to be objective, much less feel compassion for the perpetrator of their grief and loss. I had always thought that our system of public justice was designed to replace and transcend an outmoded system of private retribution with a more objective assessment of public costs and benefits. Making victims the ultimate arbiters of which criminals live or die is a radical transformation in our system of public justice and one which imposes tremendous costs impacting the quality of justice we dispense in noncapital cases as well.

My second charge of bankruptcy is a fiscal one. The most dramatic effect of Proposition 8 was the impact it had on our prison population in California. Since 1982, we have tripled the number of prisoners confined in our penal institutions. California now ranks number one in a nation that ranks number one in the world in the size of our prison population and sixteenth in the nation in the proportion of our population confined in our prisons. We have invested $6 billion to build new prison facilities, some of which remained vacant because we could not fund the staff to open them. It has been estimated that we will have to invest another five billion to achieve a level of 130 percent of capacity. None of this has much to do with the level of crime in California, nor are California citizens much safer as a result. Most of those who are confined are inner-city minorities with drug problems. The proportion of our prison population who are ethnic minorities has grown in the past decade from 64 percent to 70 percent of our prison population. It now costs about $35,000 per year to keep each inmate confined, more than the annual cost of attending California's best universities.

To a great extent, California's prisons are the universities that will graduate future generations of violent criminals. In 1989, Governor Deukmejian appointed a Blue Ribbon Commission (hereinafter "the Commission") to study the problem of inmate population management in California. The Commission was a model of how the process of reform of the criminal justice system should proceed, drawing on a broad cross section of prosecutors, judges, correctional experts, law enforcement, and even a former inmate. District Attorney Grover Trask of Riverside County served as the chairperson. After hearing the experts and exhaustive analysis of the data, this is the predominant conclusion upon which the commission unanimously agreed: The criminal justice system in California is out of balance and will remain so unless the entire state and local criminal justice system is addressed from prevention through discharge of jurisdiction. Judges and parole authorities lack sufficient intermediate sanctions to make balanced public safety decisions. What the Commission found was that too often a sentencing judge has only two alternatives: (1) lock 'em up in state prison or (2) turn 'em loose in a system of probation supervision, which is essentially meaningless because caseloads are so high. Further finding that more intermediate alternatives were needed, the Commission concluded that we could actually save money in the long run without compromising public safety. The Commission's recommendations went nowhere. They were greeted with deafening silence and have generated about as much excitement as flatulence in a friary. The reason, obviously, is because implementing these recommendations would require an immediate investment; and the savings would only be realized in the long run. We no longer make decisions of public policy based on long-term investment. We can only see as far ahead as the next election.

My third charge of bankruptcy is the moral bankruptcy of our political leadership. Some call it the Willie Horton syndrome, where political leaders with ambitions for higher office become so obsessed with maintaining a "tough on crime" image that they measure every decision in terms of the media labels that might be hung around their necks. The strongest evidence of this obsession is the national decline in the exercise of the pardon and commutation power by American

GERALD F. UELMEN

governors. During the ten-year period of 1961–1970, when we carried out 135 executions in the United States, American governors commuted 183 death sentences. During the ten years from 1980–1990, we executed 120, with fewer than sixty commutations, most of those granted by lame-duck governors who were not running for reelection. Here in California, the Willie Horton syndrome is exacting a high cost indeed. The governor's power to review paroles is being implemented like a naval blockade to prevent any prisoner from being released on parole. Governor Deukmejian's Blue Ribbon Commission's recommendations to provide some alternatives to prison sentences have run into a gubernatorial brick wall. On five occasions, the legislature has passed measures to implement those recommendations. On five occasions, they have been vetoed by the governor.

I return to my opening premise, the power of labels. The victims' rights movement has clearly demonstrated the potent political power of labels. Labels are a great way to get elected or to get initiatives enacted. However, when it comes to the hard choices—the rational search for solutions and the realistic assessment of costs versus benefits—labels become an impediment and lead to intellectual, fiscal, and moral bankruptcy. And that is precisely where our system of criminal justice is today in California—bankrupt.

---

* From *St. John's Journal of Legal Commentary,* vol. 8, p. 197 (1992–1993).

4

Leaks, Gags, and Shields*

D ISCUSSIONS OF THE impact of publicity upon trials usually begin with an analysis of rights. The defendant has a right to a fair trial. The lawyer has a right to speak. The public has a right to know. The fact that we have a right to do something, however, does not mean it is the right thing to do. In exploring the ethical dimensions of trial publicity, I would like to focus on the concept of responsibility rather than rights. How do we get the participants in a trial to accept responsibility for what they say to the media? How do we get the media to accept responsibility for what they report? My experience in high-profile trials suggests that much of what the participants say and what the media report are simply irresponsible. They act irresponsibly because the system frequently rewards their irresponsibility with high ratings or increased circulation and rarely imposes costs or consequences upon it.

The ideal of fairness that drives our adversary system of justice assumes that a verdict must be based upon evidence that is admissible in a court of law. The facts should be decided by a jury sworn to put aside any bias or prejudice, to consider only the admissible evidence, and to ignore the pressures of public opinion. But it has never been assumed that we can maintain our courts as air-sealed vacuums that will never be contaminated by public opinion. The traditional safeguards we have relied upon to ensure the ability of jurors to put aside bias or prejudice are voir dire questioning (to inspect the "baggage" jurors bring with them), challenges for cause (to remove jurors who are biased), changes of venue (to move the location of the trial), and sequestration (to insulate jurors from pervasive publicity). Contrary to popular impressions, these tools are not designed to supply us with jurors who are completely ignorant of a high-profile case but rather to assist us in finding jurors who remain skeptical, who are truly willing to suspend judgment until they have evaluated the evidence. Rather than enhancing these traditional safeguards to make them more effective, however, the modern trend is to devalue and dismantle them on the grounds they consume too much time, are too expensive, or are too invasive and burdensome for jurors. Instead, we have focused our attention upon a largely futile effort to control the flow of information to the media. Rules have been formulated to prevent lawyers from commenting upon pending cases. Laws have been enacted to punish witnesses who sell their stories. Judges have formulated gag orders to silence trial participants and occasionally have held reporters in contempt for refusing to identify their sources. Rather than suppress the barrage of publicity surrounding high-profile cases, however, these efforts more often spur the media to a relentless pursuit of even more questionable sources of information. The greatest danger to our ideal of fair trials has now become the nameless and faceless leaker of information whom we see quoted as "a source close to the investigation" or "a knowledgeable member of the defense team."

Rather than seeking to suppress identifiable sources of information, our goal should be to encourage the flow of information to the public that is attributed to an identified source who takes public responsibility for its accuracy and appropriateness. The public, including potential jurors, will then be better equipped to critically evaluate the information and assess its reliability and credibility. The approach currently utilized by our courts frequently diminishes the flow of information attributed to identified sources and increases the flow of information coming from unidentified leaks. Current "shield laws" encourage the leaking of information by protecting the leaker from any consequences for his breach of confidentiality and place no responsibility on reporters for lack of restraint in promising confidentiality to their sources. Somehow the irony has escaped us, that we encourage irresponsible breaches of confidentiality by guaranteeing to violators that we will protect the confidentiality of their breach! Those who have no respect for confidentiality that protects others are rewarded by our guarantee of absolute confidentiality for their treachery.

It is possible to identify the kinds of information that actually present a clear and present danger to the fairness of trials if prematurely released. This information will fall into very narrow categories of highly probative evidence that may be excluded at trial. Courts can and should issue protective orders to preserve the confidentiality of such information. Once protective orders are issued, courts should rigorously enforce them. Trial participants should be severely disciplined for unauthorized leaks of information included in protective orders. Courts can and should employ the contempt power to punish those responsible for the publication of such information, and shield laws should not protect the identity of those who leak it.

It is unrealistic, however, to attempt to purge trials of any trace of external publicity. The advocacy of lawyers and other trial participants cannot be confined to the courtroom. An objective of complete separation of a court of law from the court of public opinion is unattainable, and we should readily admit that it cannot be achieved. The level of public interest in high-profile trials simply cannot be controlled, and the media will inevitably respond with whatever information is available. We cannot begin to fathom all the subtle ways in which public opinion seeps into a courtroom and affects the attitudes of every participant in a trial. The traditional tools of voir dire, challenges for cause, changes of venue, and sequestration deserve greater respect and attention as our best safeguards against media intrusion. Acceptance of this reality, however, does not mean that we cannot achieve a more modest goal of delaying public disclosure of truly critical information until its admissibility has been determined in the courtroom. The public is more sophisticated and discerning in sorting out the available information than we generally give it credit for. It will usually be aided in that process by identification of the source of the information it is receiving. The message we should send to trial participants is not to be silent. The lawyers, police officers, or victims standing on the courthouse steps in front of television cameras are not the gravest danger to our ideal of fair trials. The gravest danger is the faceless and nameless "leak." The message we need to deliver to trial participants is to stand up and take responsibility for public statements. The message we should send to the media is not to report less. It is to report responsibly, to resort to unidentified sources only when the information being reported is not protected by a court order and the source is lawfully entitled to release the information. And the message we should send to our courts is to deploy traditional tools more effectively to insulate the finders of fact from external influences.

Trial participants who speak for public consumption do so for a variety of reasons. Identifying those reasons will assist in assessing the value of public attribution of their statements. Start with the police conducting an investigation. They are ordinarily the first source of information about a pending case. What motivates them in deciding what information to provide to the media? First, they may want to reassure a nervous populace that a culprit has been identified or apprehended to relieve community tension. While expressions of confidence they have the right person may be inconsistent with a presumption of innocence, prospective jurors are fully capable of understanding that police confidence in the guilt of an arrested person is not itself persuasive evidence of guilt. Second, police may want to enlist public assistance in ongoing investigative efforts to locate victims, witnesses, or evidence. Third, they may want to influence public opinion about their own competence to increase public confidence they are doing a good job. Fourth, they may want to enhance the prospect of a successful prosecution by increasing public confidence in a suspect's guilt. Finally, they may be advancing some personal agenda by earning or returning media favor. Prosecutors may share any and all the motives of the police. Public apprehension may find greater relief with an announcement that charges have been filed than with a police announcement of an arrest. The need for public assistance may not end when the prosecution commences. Public confidence that one is doing a good job becomes especially important to one whose office is elective. The enhancement of prospects for ultimate conviction may also become a more powerful motivator since the prosecutor will be personally identified with the win or loss. And prosecutors will have personal agendas to earn or return media favor too. A high-profile case may be a stepping-stone to a judgeship, another elective office, or even a media career. In addition to the motives they share with police, prosecutors may have tactical motives for releasing information that they believe will influence the way the case is handled by others. Their real purpose may not be to inform the public, but to convey a message to the judge or to opposing counsel. They may also be trying to increase the odds that questionable evidence will be admitted by the judge at trial. A trial judge is well aware that a claim that the defendant was prejudiced by the release of evidence prior to trial will be rendered "harmless error" if the evidence is later admitted. The admissibility of evidence at trial is frequently a close question left to the discretion of the trial judge. Prosecutors know that the trial judge's eagerness to compile a trial record inviting affirmance by a higher court may push the judge in the direction of admitting evidence that was released prior to trial to foreclose any claim that the pretrial release prejudiced the defendant.

Defense lawyers who are representing a client may believe that a variety of the interests of the client will be served by the public release of information. First, of course, they may want to enhance the prospects of a favorable disposition of the case by creating public sympathy for their client or doubts about the prosecution's case. The opportunity to create sympathy for the defendant may be greater than the opportunity presented at the trial itself since offering "good character" evidence at trial opens the door for the prosecution to offer evidence of "bad character." The planting of doubts involves very traditional tools of advocacy. If a reporter calls and asks for a comment on a story that new evidence of your client's guilt has been exposed, the defense lawyer will want the story to include the reasons the evidence might be mistrusted, such as the bias of a witness or the possibility of a mistake. A revelation of damning evidence accompanied by the observation that the defendant's lawyer had "no comment" will simply enhance the credibility of the story. Second, the defense lawyer may share a client's concern for his reputation or public image apart from the pending charges. A client who is never prosecuted or one who is prosecuted and acquitted may have been ill served by a lawyer who allowed public speculation about his guilt to go unchallenged. Security guard Richard Jewell, for example, was subjected to intensive media speculation regarding FBI suspicions of his involvement in the bombing at Atlanta's Centennial Park during the 1986 Summer Olympic Games. Third, defense lawyers may want to send public messages to the police, the prosecutors, the witnesses, or the judge for some tactical reason. Occasionally, defense lawyers are pursuing the public agenda of some organization other than their client. The role of the Communist Party in the defense of the Scottsboro Boys comes to mind. And of course, defense lawyers are certainly motivated by personal agendas, such as self-aggrandizement. Not only is free advertising hard to resist, there may be a book deal or a screen play waiting in the wings or even a new career as a television commentator. Most rarely of all, a defense lawyer may be financing the case by the sale of information. Such an arrangement creates a serious conflict of interest, but one that some courts have permitted the client to waive. While lawyers rarely welcome the defendant himself as a public spokesperson, the phenomenon of celebrity defendants or corporate defendants hiring a public relations consultant to handle trial publicity is not unheard of. Their motive is rarely ambiguous. Jeopardy to investments of millions of dollars may depend upon "damage control." Consider, for example, the costly impact upon the career of a media star posed with sexual misconduct or child molestation charges. While charges may never be filed, confidential investigative reports are frequently leaked to the media.

The O. J. Simpson trials brought to the spotlight dozens of other trial participants with their own motives to influence public opinion. Family members of the defendant stepped forward to defend his character from personal attack, while family members of the victims were anxious to rebut any public disparagement of their loved ones. The victims' rights movement has done much to transform our concept of public justice into a system of private retribution, and we should not have any illusions that the voice given to previously voiceless victims will only be heard in the courtroom. The media has discovered that victims and their families are a compelling presence in trial coverage. Even witnesses may be motivated to capitalize on their newfound celebrity. The payment of cash to witnesses for exclusive rights to their "stories" has become a common practice of the tabloid media. While the receipt of such payments has now been made criminal in California, there are reasons to doubt the enforceability of this prohibition. In any event, the siren's song of instant celebrity may be a more powerful inducement to some witnesses than cash, especially if they see some way to convert their celebrity to cash later.

When we sort through the myriad of motives that lead police, prosecutors, defense lawyers, defendants, victims, and witnesses to become news sources, we can readily distinguish those objectives that are served by speaking for attribution from those served by surreptitious leaks. The appropriate goals of assuaging public fears or enlisting public assistance or projecting an image of competence will best be served by public announcements from a readily identifiable spokesperson. The questionable goal of enhancing the prospects for conviction or acquittal may be better served by leaks. The sleazy process of currying media favor will usually be better served by leaks since giving anyone an "exclusive" in a statement for public attribution usually makes more enemies than friends. A well-placed leak makes a friend and leaves potential enemies not knowing whom to hate. Criminal defense lawyers sometimes have to contend with a "sleaze" factor that police and prosecutors do not ordinarily face. Information from an unidentified source may sometimes have greater credibility than a public announcement from a criminal defense lawyer. The presumptions that apply to police and prosecutors might even be reversed for defense lawyers. The personal agendas are achieved by public statements. Meanwhile, the goal of undermining public confidence in a client's guilt or preserving his reputation is often effectively served by leaks. This offers no justification for leaking, however. It merely magnifies the harm the leak imposes by depriving the public of the means to assess the credibility of information. Lawyers remain advocates for their clients in the "court" of public opinion, and it is appropriate that the public take their advocacy role into account in assessing the credibility of their statements.

From an ethical perspective, it is hard to imagine a scenario in which the use of surreptitious leaks by a lawyer directly involved in a case can be justified. A defense lawyer may argue that his or her chief obligation is to advance the cause of the client, and the choice of whether to issue a statement for public attribution or to leak information to the press is simply a tactical choice driven by whichever better serves the interests of the client. But the defense lawyer's advocacy has always been limited by the constraints of what the law allows. The law certainly does not allow the surreptitious leaking of information that presents a clear and present danger to the fairness of the trial nor does it permit leaking of information included in a protective order issued by a court. While the law does allow a lawyer to be an advocate for his client in the public forum, there should be no hesitation to say that an advocate must "enter an appearance" in the court of public opinion, just as he must enter an appearance in court. If we are going to recognize the right of a lawyer to enter the arena of public opinion on behalf of a client, why should we hesitate to demand that he identify himself as the source of information so the public can accurately assess his credibility? The exceptional circumstances where public advocacy is permitted but the client's interest might be better served by anonymity do not justify vesting lawyers with discretion to speak anonymously that more frequently will be exercised to serve their own interests.

For prosecutors, whose only appropriate justification for leaking can be the public interest, the balance is easier to cast: the public interest will always be better served by identification of the source of information. It would be naïveté of the highest order to suggest that opening the door to public statements by trial participants will close the door to surreptitious leaking. Even when trial participants feel perfectly free to speak for attribution, they will have reasons to prefer to remain anonymous. The reasons to remain anonymous, however, will rarely be reasons that serve the public interest or the cause of justice. From an ethical perspective, attribution should be preferred since it gives the public vital information necessary to evaluate the weight to be given the information. Concealing the identity of the source conceals the motives and agendas for its release. Those motives and agendas relate directly to credibility. Too often, the choice of attribution or anonymity is left completely to the source. Few journalists apparently ponder the ethical consequences of that choice or approach it from any perspective other than how best to get someone to "open up." The new Code of Ethics of the Society of Professional Journalists invites journalists to approach the choice of attribution or anonymity from an ethical perspective: Identify sources whenever feasible. The public is entitled to as much information as possible on sources' reliability. Always question sources' motives before promising anonymity. Clarify conditions attached to any promise made in exchange for information. Keep promises. Avoid undercover or other surreptitious methods of gathering information except when traditional open methods will not yield information vital to the public. Use of such methods should be explained as part of the story.

Journalists are known to occasionally laugh at the concept of "legal ethics" as an oxymoron. It seems fair to ask whether "responsible journalism" is also an inherent contradiction. The real problem in defining a code of ethics to govern journalists is that there is no longer any agreement upon who is a "journalist," if there ever was. In 1926, when Sigma Delta Chi, the Society of Professional Journalists, first promulgated a code of ethics, journalists were generally thought of as newspaper reporters. While ferreting out news stories was a highly competitive enterprise back then, newspaper reporters knew who their competitors were. They were the reporters who worked for other newspapers. Today, consider all the sources of information about a pending trial. Most Americans rely for most of their news upon television news shows. A debate continues to rage among journalists whether television news is a venture in journalism or simply public entertainment. The print media divides itself between "legitimate" press and the "tabloid" press. What distinguishes the tabloids is not just their means of gathering stories (they pay cash), but the nature of the stories that interest them. For them, "public interest" and "prurient interest" mean the same thing. Now the "tabloid" television shows have created a similar division between "legitimate" television news reporters and shows such as *Hard Copy* and *A Current Affair*. And then what do you do with the talk shows? The outrageous is highly valued because it provokes a reaction. Is Rush Limbaugh a journalist? Is Geraldo Rivera?

The journalist's ethic of protecting confidential sources of information should not be left completely in the hands of each individual journalist to define. Other contexts in which confidentiality is protected by an evidentiary privilege require an express or implied promise of confidentiality to serve some publicly recognized goal. A communication to a priest, a physician, or a lawyer would not be legally protected simply because the recipient promised confidentiality if the confidentiality were not related to the publicly recognized goal of administering spiritual counseling, medical treatment, or legal advice. Each of these privileges is also limited by exceptions, such as the one for communications to further a criminal venture. As with any other professional, journalists should be subjected to limits upon their ability to guarantee confidentiality to news sources. One appropriate limit would be a caveat that sources such as lawyers, witnesses, police, and other participants in pending court proceedings cannot be utilized as sources without attribution if doing so violates a valid protective order or a rule of professional conduct of their own profession.

---

* From "Leaks, Gags and Shields: Taking Responsibility," *Santa Clara Law Review*, vol. 37, p. 943 (1997).

5

Ruminations on Fixing the System

TOILING IN THE trenches of the American criminal justice system for half a century, I have long abandoned any illusions that criminal justice policy is the product of rational analysis. It is the product of media hype and political slugfests in which fear of crime is manipulated to defeat candidates who are perceived as "soft" on crime. But I saw faint glimmers of hope in recent measures ameliorating harsh drug laws. Obama's Fair Sentencing Act reduced the ratio between crack and powder cocaine for purposes of federal mandatory minimum sentences from the ridiculous one hundred to one down to the preposterous eighteen to one. The momentum of the push to decriminalize marijuana suggests that drug hype may have declining influence. A 2014 California initiative (Proposition 47) eliminated prosecutorial and judicial discretion to treat many nonviolent drug offenses as felonies. However, Marie Gottschalk, in her recent analysis of our prison state (*Caught: The Prison State and the Lockdown of American Politics*, Princeton University Press, 2015), disabuses us of the notion that winding down the drug war will dramatically reduce our prison and jail populations. Noting that the prison state has extended its reach to other marginalized groups (including immigrants, poor whites, and those charged with sex offenses), she convincingly demonstrates the following:

> For those seeking to dismantle the carceral state, the key challenge is not to determine what specific sentencing and other reforms would slash the number of people in jail and prison. The real challenge is figuring out how to create a political environment that is more receptive to such reforms and how to make the far-reaching

consequences of the carceral state into a leading political and public policy issue.

In many states, restrictions on where convicted sex offenders can live have left homelessness as their only alternative. The political clout of unions of correctional officers and police in many states outweighs the influence of teachers' unions. The overcrowding of prisons, the abandonment of any pretense of rehabilitation, and the privatization of jails and prisons have eroded the conditions of confinement to levels of shameful inhumanity.

In 1884, John Peter Altgeld, who as governor of Illinois later ordained his political demise by pardoning the Haymarket "anarchists," published a remarkable little volume titled *Our Penal Machinery and Its Victims*. Identifying the same flaws in the prison state of a century ago that remain present in today's, his solution was indeterminate sentencing, which would motivate prisoners to "reform" in order to shorten their sentences. A century later, California was among the states that abandoned indeterminate sentencing, finding it was fundamentally flawed in its confidence that the risks of recidivism could be assessed based on a prisoner's behavior while confined. The governor who presided over that reform has been resurrected in California, and in response to a 2011 U.S. Supreme Court ruling that the conditions of confinement in California were unconstitutional, Jerry Brown presided over a massive "realignment" to move prisoners out of the state prisons and into county jails for shorter terms. Since then, California has approved applications from twenty-one counties to build more than ten thousand new jail beds at a cost of $1.2 billion, and counties have eschewed using the billions of new state dollars allocated for realignment to invest in mental health and substance abuse treatment and other social services for the offenders diverted out of the state prison system. We are on the verge of squandering the opportunity that realignment offered.

The gap that divides the rich from the poor seems to get wider every year—not just in the United States, but throughout the world. Somehow we have lost sight of the concept of a good education, decent health care, and access to justice as basic human rights to which every person is entitled. Even the promise of *Gideon v. Wainwright*—that indigent accused are entitled to competent representation by counsel— is becoming more elusive. Budgets for indigent defense and support for public defender offices remain easy targets when we have to rein in spending. Wrapping them in the flag of constitutional protection doesn't seem to get us very far. We need to understand that we are all stakeholders in having a population that is well educated, healthy, and feels they are fairly treated by the system.

Among my greatest disappointments is that while we have apparently produced a surplus of lawyers, so few of them can afford to take on the representation of those who can only afford modest fees or no fees at all. In California, over 80 percent of those seeking divorces are now unrepresented. Every day, thousands are told that even though they can prove they were cheated out of thousands of dollars, the cost of going to court to right the wrong forecloses relief. We need recognition that a right to competent representation should apply to civil proceedings as well as criminal trials. The efforts to make competent representation available to indigents in civil cases have met intransigent political opposition. Justice Earl Johnson, a hero in the movement to extend the availability of civil legal services to all, remains pessimistic after a lifetime of effort: "Based on its history so far," he writes, "it seems justice for lower-income people in the United States may remain forever in jeopardy. . . . Stable one year and teetering on the brink the next. Yet it appears it may be ever thus."

IV

Reflections on
Educating Lawyers

1

Why Go to Law School?*

IN 1986, UPON my appointment as dean of Santa Clara University School of Law, I welcomed my first incoming class with the following remarks:

While comic strips are frequently a source of amusement, they occasionally raise provocative questions that make us uncomfortable. A couple of months ago, Charles Schulz raised a very provocative question for us in *Peanuts*. The strip depicts Snoopy as a lawyer, with briefcase and bowler hat, being confronted by Linus, the polite little kid who is remarkably gifted with profound philosophical insights. Linus asks a question which I'm sure every one of you in this room has been asked, or will be asked: "If there are already 700,000 attorneys in this country, why do we need you?" Snoopy walks away, thinking "Attorneys hate questions like that."

That's not a question we can walk away from today, as we welcome 260 of you to your first day of law school. Let's explore how you might respond to such a hard question.

The easiest way to answer Linus' question might be to employ the Socratic technique of law professors: respond by asking another question. You might ask, "How many senior citizens were evicted or denied social security benefits last year without ever seeing a lawyer?" Or, "How many undocumented immigrants are deported every day without the assistance of counsel?"

The risk of employing this technique is that your questioner might employ the same technique and ask you still another question. "Are *you* planning to devote your legal career to the representation of the infirm aged or indigent immigrants?" I would hope some of you could answer that question affirmatively without hedging, but I harbor no illusion that a majority would do so.

Another approach to Linus' question is to challenge his premise. While there are 700,000 attorneys in this country, they are not evenly distributed. New York and San Francisco may be abundantly supplied, but many smaller communities and rural areas still have real needs.

This answer may suffer the same drawback as the first. Many of you are at Santa Clara Law School because you hope to pursue your legal career in the Bay Area, and perceive that Santa Clara's local reputation will make such a transition easier. While your perception is certainly accurate, I hope you will take advantage of the broader horizons our placement office can offer. Fully satisfying legal careers can be readily found in smaller communities, offering their own set of rewards. Those rewards won't include $100,000 the first year out, though.

Still another approach to the query might be to utilize the glib comeback. Examples include, "We'll always need more *good* lawyers." Or, "We can certainly use more *ethical* lawyers." While few will take issue with such sentiments, they tend to be tautological. With rare exceptions, the 700,000 lawyers who preceded you to the bar can also describe themselves with complete justification as good, ethical lawyers. Joining in the denigration of our profession and mindless condemnation of our peers is hardly an appropriate justification for seeking to join their ranks.

You might justify your lawyerly ambitions by highlighting the ways in which you *are* different from your 700,000 future peers. Over 40 percent of you are women, and only 15% of the profession is female. Twenty percent of you represent ethnic minorities, and your addition to the professional rolls will offset the gross underrepresentation of your group.

Unquestionably, we are still playing "catch up" in the effort to open the legal profession to all segments of our society. That still leaves most of you without an answer, though. And I hope that many of you are uncomfortable with a response that simply suggests, "You need me because I'm a woman, or because I'm black, brown or yellow."

The most satisfying answer to the question of why we need you might be suggested in Snoopy's lack of response to Linus. Snoopy's failure to reply is a dead giveaway. It unmasks Snoopy as a fraud.

Snoopy is not a real attorney. Snoopy thinks "Attorneys hate questions like that." You don't hate questions like that. I don't hate questions like that. Lawyers *like* hard questions. And that's precisely why we need more lawyers.

We live in a world which provides lots of hard questions to be answered. We have plenty of people around to offer easy answers that won't survive hard analysis. You're going to spend the next three or four years struggling with many of the hardest questions you've ever been asked. You're going to acquire analytical skills that are demanding and rigorous. Those of you who master those skills will always be needed.

Today, a legal education offers a broader array of career choices than ever before. Even those who pursue careers in the business world will find their law degree is a substantial asset. With so many lawyers to deal with, corporate America is seeking executives who can think like lawyers, and tackle the tough questions with lawyer-like analysis. Unlike Snoopy, real lawyers don't simply walk away from hard questions. They struggle for answers. Welcome to what I hope will be a lifetime of struggle for you. We do need you.

---

*   Commentary, "Why Does the Country Need 260 Additional Lawyers?" *San Jose Mercury News,* August 25, 1986, p. 5B.

2

Welcome to Cardozo's Crowd*

I N 1993, I presented the following remarks to graduates of Santa
Clara Law School who had passed the bar examination and were
being sworn in as members of the bar:

> Admission to the bar may be the fulfillment of a lifelong dream.
> But it does not mean your struggles are over. You now discover the
> truth of Justice Benjamin Cardozo's admonition that the life of a
> lawyer "is no life of cloistered ease. This is a life that you must live
> in the crowd."
>
> The crowd continues to grow. With the 1993 crop, we have
> nearly 141,000 lawyers eligible to practice law in California. You are
> entering the profession in a period of the most intense competition for
> starting positions we have ever seen. The uncertainty of our economic
> times may seem to many of you a cruel trick of fate, coming just at
> the point when you've achieved the goal you've worked so hard to
> achieve. I ask you to view the hard times in which you enter our
> profession from another perspective, the perspective of history.
>
> If we look back at what period in our history was the most
> exciting moment to be entering the legal profession, one would have
> to say it was the period of our darkest economic uncertainty, the early
> 1930's. As the populist historian Page Smith put it:
>
>> The most interesting aspect of any society is where
>> its creative energies flow, what class of profession assumes
>> the burden of service and redemption. For the "rising
>> generation" of the '30s it would plainly be the lawyers, first
>> as practitioners and teachers, and then as judges, interpreting
>> the law.

While economic hard times may destroy some of the illusions you might have had about the legal profession as an elite sanctuary of economic independence, that illusion may be supplanted with a reality which is much more satisfying. In times of economic hardship, Americans have always found a new capacity to share what they have, to offer a helping hand to those less fortunate, and to take consolation from the fact that we are all in the same boat, and will rise or fall together. It kind of brings us back to our beginnings, when our ancestors first got off the boat.

One of the first to arrive was a lawyer. His name was John Winthrop, and he expressed this ideal as well as it has ever been expressed. He said: "It is God's intention that every person might have need of another, and from hence they might be knit together in the bonds of affection. We must be knit together in this work as one. We must delight in each other, make others' condition our own."

The way out of the economic morass we find ourselves in is not to step over each other, but to reassert the value of community, of mutual love and of caring for the needs of others.

Lately, I've heard lots of lawyers complaining about "what's wrong with the legal profession." Many comment that practicing law isn't as much fun as it used to be. Frequently these complaints simply reveal a lack of perspective. We tend to assume that our "profession" is an amorphous entity that doesn't respond to our personal goals or our personal pain. Life as a lawyer can be very stressful if we perceive our fellow lawyers as simply part of Cardozo's "crowd," rather than fellow human beings with whom we must live in relationship.

You each have the power to define for yourselves the profession in which you live and work. A new license to practice law bestows enormous power to affect the lives of others. What is often overlooked is the power you started out with, the power to make harmony and unity in your own lives.

Can you find a life of harmony and unity in the legal profession? In searching for my own answer to that question, I discovered that precisely the same question was asked of Oliver Wendell Holmes, Jr., 100 years ago. The question was asked in this form: "How can I reach my own spiritual possibilities through a door such as this? How can the laborious study of a dry and technical system, the greedy watch for clients and the practice of shopkeepers' arts, the mannerless conflicts over often sordid interests, make out a life?"

I don't think I can improve on the answer that Holmes gave to that question: "If you have the soul of an idealist, you will make your world ideal. . . . One may live greatly in the law as well as elsewhere. Here as well as elsewhere your thought may find its unity in an infinite perspective; here as well as elsewhere you may drink the bitter cup of heroism, and may wear out your heart after the unattainable."

If I might paraphrase Holmes, if you have the soul of a cynic, you will make a cynical world of greed and self-interest. What we've tried to nurture at Santa Clara are the souls of idealists, and one need not sell that soul to enter the door you pass through today.

In the course of the past eight years, I have participated in admission ceremonies for nearly 2,000 graduates of Santa Clara Law. I can't say that every one of them found a comfortable life of satisfaction and fulfillment in the practice of law. But that's not the true measure of success. The success we strive for is nothing less than a world of peace and harmony, in which the dignity and worth of all persons is valued, and the liberties we cherish, and the justice we pursue, are available to all. I'm confident that your admission to the bar will bring us a step closer to achieving that goal.

---

*   "Reflections on Being a Lawyer," *San Francisco Daily Journal,* December 30, 1993, p.4.

3

The Virtuous Lawyer

T HE FOLLOWING REMARKS were delivered as the commencement address for the graduates of the final class I served as dean at Santa Clara University School of Law on May 21, 1994:

Among the best sellers this past year was a book by William Bennett III entitled *The Book of Virtues*. Classic stories offer inspiring examples of ten virtues, such as honesty, loyalty, and courage. As I read through the stories, however, I was disappointed to find very few stories by or about lawyers. It was a bit like the Irish gentleman wandering through a cemetery who saw a headstone that read "Here lies a lawyer and a virtuous man." He said, "And who'd ever think there'd be room for two men in that little grave?"

As I thought about the reasons that might explain the short supply of stories about virtuous lawyers, it occurred to me that Bennett left out some of the virtues we stress most in the formation of lawyers. A "book of virtues" devoted to the virtues of skepticism or persistence or self-confidence would certainly be filled with inspiring examples from the legal profession.

One reason these may not be perceived as lawyerly virtues is that they are so frequently manifested in their exaggerated form as the parallel vices of cynicism, obstinacy, and arrogance. The virtues that make a lawyer loved, when carried to extreme, become the vices that make a lawyer hated.

Let's start with skepticism. Skepticism is the fundamental virtue introduced to you during your first week of law school. All of the assumptions you brought with you in your baggage were questioned. You began to doubt whether you even owned the clothes you were wearing. Judge Learned Hand, who has been described as the greatest judge who never sat on the Supreme Court, equated skepticism with the spirit of liberty—the spirit, as he put it, that is not too sure it is right. Grant Gilmore in *The Ages of American Law* told us, "The function of the lawyer is to preserve a skeptical relativism in a society hell-bent for absolutes."

Good lawyers are rarely surprised because good lawyers are rarely certain about anything. And a good judge remains skeptical even about her own previous precedents, ready to overrule them when persuaded they are wrong.

While skepticism is a virtue for both the good lawyer and the good judge, at some point, it can be tragically transformed to cynicism. Henry L. Stimson, a lawyer who served in the cabinets of five presidents, once said, "The only deadly sin I know is cynicism."

Cynicism is such a deadly sin because it transforms the entire landscape to the color gray. Lawyers spend much of their lives convincing others that things are gray rather than black or white. The chief hazard of spending your life convincing others that everything is gray is that you will convince yourself and become the ultimate victim of your own craft. Oscar Wilde described a cynic as one who knows the price of everything and the value of nothing. Unlike the skeptic, who constantly seeks evidence before reaching a tentative conclusion, the cynic begins with a conclusion and questions only the motives of those who dispute it.

The second lawyerly virtue I want to discuss is persistence. You have all seen examples in your law school studies of arguments that were presented again and again, year after year, gaining in persuasive power until they prevailed and became established principles of law. The most inspiring example is the lifelong struggle of Charles Houston and Thurgood Marshall to challenge the separate-but-equal doctrine that sustained a century of racial injustice.

Justice Louis Brandeis once said, "Persistency is the jewel." The life of Brandeis is itself a jewel of perseverance. As a justice, his persistent dissents created momentum for monumental legal changes. Did he ever get discouraged and want to give up? Of course. Once when his daughter complained that a task was too difficult, Brandeis was heard saying, "My dear, if you will just start with the idea that this is a hard world, it will all be much simpler." That's good advice for those about to launch a legal career. Include among your goals some that will take a lifetime of persistence to achieve in a hard world.

At some point, though, can persistence become a vice? When does our obsession with the seemingly unobtainable simply become obstinacy? It's no answer to say, as Sir Thomas Brown said, "Obstinacy in a bad cause is but constancy in a good cause." The virtue of persistence cannot be transformed to the vice of obstinacy simply by the label we put on the cause asserted. The difference lies in the will, the heart, and the mind—not in the cause. That's a lesson Shakespeare taught in *Hamlet*:

> To persevere in obstinate condolement is a curse of impious stubbornness; It shows a will most incorrect to heaven, a heart unfortified, a mind impatient.

The obstinate lawyer or judge may simply be a persistent lawyer or judge who lacks the virtue of skepticism, unwilling to even consider the possible merit of opposing arguments. Just as our virtues frequently reinforce each other, our vices are often complementary.

The third lawyerly virtue in my trinity is self-confidence—that quiet, assured feeling you have just before you fall flat on your face. This, of course, is a virtue for any calling; but it has a special place in the practice of law. When clients place their lives and fortunes in your hands, when you first face an adversary who is just as motivated to prevail as you are, you will experience fear. But as Eleanor Roosevelt reassures us, "You gain strength, courage, and confidence by every experience in which you really stop to look fear in the face."

As your confidence grows, you may reach a point at which the virtue of confidence is transformed to the vice of arrogance. That's a crucial point for a lawyer, so let me see if I can define it with greater precision.

It is the point Donald Regan reached when he became chief of staff of the White House and said, "I'm not arrogant. I just believe there's no human problem that couldn't be solved—if people would simply do as I tell 'em."

It's the point William Gladstone reached when he became prime minister of England, and Henry Labouchere commented, "I do not object to Gladstone always having the ace of trumps up his sleeve, but merely to his belief that God Almighty put it there."

Unfortunately, it's the point too many judges reach, believing that their elevation to the bench is akin to an ascension to divinity. Frequently, the arrogant lawyer or judge is simply seeking to deflate the confidence of other lawyers and judges. Remember that and don't let the arrogance of others diminish your own self-confidence as a lawyer. Again, I turn to Eleanor Roosevelt's advice on that score: "No one can make you feel inferior without your consent."

We can see that the line that separates skepticism from cynicism, that separates persistence from obstinacy, and that separates self-confidence from arrogance is a matter of degree. We're obviously not talking about the degree you were awarded this morning. We're talking about the unseen degrees that the poet John Dryden was describing when he wrote, "Ill habits gather by unseen degrees—As brooks make rivers, rivers run to seas."

Are there safeguards we can rely upon to sound an alarm when we venture across the line that marks the cynical, the obstinate, and the arrogant? I would suggest three: they are friendship, humor, and reflection.

The friendship of which I speak is not the sense in which friendship is normally spoken of today. I speak of a more traditional concept that was aptly described by Robert Bellah in his wonderful book, *The Habits of the Heart*. Let me borrow his description:

> The traditional idea of friendship put forward by Aristotle . . . had three essential components. Friends must enjoy one another's company, they must be useful to one another, and they must share a common commitment to the good. . . . For Aristotle and his successors, it was precisely the moral component of friendship that made it the indispensable basis of a good society. For it is one of the main duties of friends to help one another to be better persons; one must hold up a standard for one's friend and be able to count on a true friend to do likewise.

As you encounter the cynical, the obstinate, and the arrogant in our profession, you will observe one sad thing they have in common. They are friendless. They have no true friends in the sense in which Robert Bellah speaks. I pray that each of you will find friends at the bar. And that you will be a friend to your fellow lawyers, the kind of friend who inspires virtue for the common good. There is an ancient expression among lawyers: "My friends at the bar." Shakespeare captured the camaraderie of lawyers thus: "Do as adversaries do in law—strive mightily, but eat and drink as friends."

The second safeguard to keep us from crossing the line from virtuous to vicious is our sense of humor. Lawyers and judges take themselves much too seriously. We need to occasionally step back from the ridiculous wrangling in which we are immersed and see the humor in the situation. One of my favorite examples of a lawyer who hasn't lost his sense of humor is Robert Jay Lifton, who wrote the poem "My Client." It extols the lawyerly virtues of skepticism, persistence, and confidence.

> Who came to me with tearful eyes, with wringing hands and piteous sighs, and swore the charges were all lies? My Client.
>
> Who promised me while still in jail, that if I got him out on bail, my fee he'd pay and would not fail? My Client.
>
> Who caused me endless pain and grief? And gave me almost no relief, from statements far beyond belief? My Client.
>
> But when at last we'd won the game, (the jury absolved him from all blame), Who shook my hand and praised my name? My Client.
>
> Then who, despite my earnest plea, laughed at me and sneered with glee, declined to pay my modest fee? My Client.
>
> Who, when I get into the mood, will be repaid for acts so rude, and get his ass . . . soundly sued? My Client.

The third safeguard for your virtue as lawyers is reflection. Just as you make time in your life for exercise to preserve your physical health, you need to make time for reflection to preserve your moral virtue. As you reflect, you may discover that poets have more to say to you than law professors or judges about how to keep your virtues from becoming vices.

The suggestion that our virtues contain the seeds of our vices is a theme that has inspired poets, and the greatest of all poets drew a lawyerly analogy to reflect on this paradox. He also spoke to us as the kind of friend Robert Bellah exhorts us to become. I want to leave you with that poet's words. William Shakespeare, Sonnet Number 35, words that were set to music several years ago by Sting in a song he entitled "Consider Me Gone."

> No more be grieved at that which thou hast done.
> Roses have thorns, and silver fountains mud,
> Clouds and eclipses strain both moon and sun,
> And loathsome canker lives in the sweetest bud.
> All men make faults, and even I in this,
> Authorizing thy trespass with compare.
> Myself corrupting, salving thy amiss,
> Excusing thy sins more than thy sins are.
> For to thy sensual fault I bring in sense,
> Thy adverse party is thy advocate—
> And 'gainst myself a lawful plea commence.
> Such civil war is in my love and hate,
> That I an accessory needs must be,
> To that sweet thief which sourly robs from me.

Thank you, God bless you, and good luck on the bar exam. Consider me gone.

GERALD F. UELMEN

4

How to Teach "Civility"*

A GREAT TRADITION of the American bar is under increasing attack. The tradition I refer to is name-calling. From the earliest inception of our profession, lawyers have been masters in the art of invective. We are frequently retained because our inarticulate clients need our voices to hurl epithets at their enemies. The greatest lawyers of the age were noted for their skill, dexterity, and wit in insulting their opponents as well as the judges who ruled against them.

Consider the argument of Cicero, the Roman orator who tried murder cases before the birth of Christ. In one of his trials, he turned to the prosecutor and said:

> Now Erucius, please do not take offence about what I am going to say next. I assure you I shall not be saying it just in order to be unpleasant, but because you need the reminder. Even if fortune has not given you the advantage of knowing for certain who your father was, which would have given you a better idea of how a father feels towards his children, at any rate nature has endowed you with your fair share of human feelings.

Or consider the reaction of Rufus Choate, the greatest lawyer in Boston during an era that included Daniel Webster, as he summed up an adverse ruling by Chief Justice Shaw:

> That judge is . . . a fool, —he can't put two ideas together . . . he's bigoted as the devil!

Now I will be the first to admit that the level of invective among lawyers has declined in quality in recent years. Consider the lawyer who turned to his opponent during a deposition and said, "You are an obnoxious little twit. Keep your mouth shut." Or consider the lawyer whose pithy response to an obnoxious letter concluded, "Fuck you. Strong letter to follow." But this decline in the erudition of our discourse should inspire a summons to greater heights of malediction.

Instead, we are hearing bar presidents and judicial committees bemoaning the decline of "civility" in our profession. Recently, the Committee on Civility of the Seventh Circuit released an interim report that placed the blame for declining civility right where it obviously belongs—in the lap of the law schools. Just as the remedy for lawyers who lied and connived across the front pages of Watergate was to require all law students to take a course in legal ethics, the committee suggested that law schools consider instituting courses in civility in the law school curriculum. That set me to thinking about what a syllabus for such a course might look like.

I think it would be appropriate to begin the course with a strong interdisciplinary note by studying the civility of discourse in other professional callings. Like baseball. Students should be exposed to these examples:

> Harry Wendelstedt: "Call me anything . . . but don't call me Durocher. A Durocher is the lowest form of living matter."
> Bugs Bear, describing outfielder Ping Bodie: "His head was full of larceny, but his feet were honest."
> Charlie Finley: "I have often called Bowie Kuhn a village idiot. I apologize to all the village idiots of America. He is the nation's idiot."
> Umpire Marty Springstead: "The best way to test a Timex would be to strap it to [Earl] Weaver's tongue.'"

We could also assign the reading of some very articulate law review articles so students could behold the contribution that legal scholars have made to the preservation of great moments in courtroom history. They could consider an article titled "Defendant Nomenclature in Criminal Trials," which collects all the appellations prosecutors have successfully affixed to criminal defendants in closing arguments. My favorite was the Missouri district attorney who suggested the defendant "ought to be shot through the mouth of a red hot cannon, through a barb wire fence into the jaws of hell," and after that, "he ought to be kicked in the seat of the pants by a Missouri mule and thrown into a manure pile to rot."

Most prosecutors seem to favor animal allusions. Cases are collected in which defendants were called dogs, hogs, hyenas, rats, rattlesnakes, skunks, vultures, wolves, and worms. James Gorman suggests that an evolutionary scale can be utilized to assess the level of disgust that animal allusions engender, noting the difference, for example, between calling Ed Meese a "dirty rat," an "insect," and a "slug":

> Part of the answer may lie in evolutionary biology. Evolutionarily, slugs are pretty distant from us, what with all our limbs and our clearly defined ears. And the further things get from us, in evolutionary terms, the creepier they seem. Other mammals may be fearsome, but they're seldom disgusting. Birds are cute. Reptiles at least aren't gooey. Amphibians are pushing it. And once you move outside of the vertebrates, it's yuck city. Insects, spiders, worms, grubs, slugs.

Another contribution to the literature of vilification is titled "A Study in Epithetical Jurisprudence." It collects every case in which someone was called a "son of a bitch." A case is reported in which the defendant sued for slander for calling the plaintiff a son of a bitch relied on the defense of truth and set out to prove that the plaintiff truly was a son of a bitch. As his final witness, he called a tall, lean suntanned gentleman to the stand. In answer to the question, "What is your business or profession?" he testified, "I am an expert judge of sons o' bitches. Out in Texas, we got a lot of 'em, and my business is knowing how to spot 'em. I can spot one a mile away on a clear day." He was then asked to carefully observe the plaintiff. He looked, turned to the jury, and said, "Gentlemen, he's a son of a bitch if I ever saw one." It calls to mind the observation Mark Twain offered in the introduction to *Pudd'nhead Wilson*. Pudd'nhead, incidentally, was a lawyer. Twain said,

> Observe the ass, for instance: his character is about perfect, he is the choicest spirit among all the humbler animals, yet see what ridicule has brought him to. Instead of feeling complimented when we are called an ass, we are left in doubt.

Pudd'nhead Wilson should be assigned reading for a course in civility. Mark Twain describes the initial debate among townspeople as to whether the young lawyer was a "fool," a "damn fool," a "lummox," a "labrick," or a "perfect jackass." They finally settled on "pudd'nhead," which stuck. While my *Funk & Wagnalls* describes a "lummox" as a stupid, clumsy person (*cf. infra*, "schlemiel"), I have been unable to find a definition of "labrick" anywhere.

Stuart Berg Flexner suggests good reason for Americans to be left in doubt when called an ass:

> Until World War II it was assumed that ass for a stupid person referred to jackass, but since 1940 it has increasingly referred to [anus], . . . (this confusion doesn't exist in England, where ass refers to the animal, arse to the part of the body).

Flexner collects and catalogues eighty-seven ways to call someone stupid, an invaluable resource for lawyers and law students. Students who seek to master the art of civil scurrility must also be exposed to the nuances of the law of libel. Use of epithets that are not capable of factual proof or disproof will receive judicial protection. Thus, the coach of the Denver Gold got away with calling a sports agent a "sleazebag who slimed up from the bayou" because it was impossible to prove whether someone is a sleazebag or not. On the other hand, recovery was allowed by a plaintiff who was called a "turkey" because this connotes "ineptitude, dumbness, and ignorance," which can be easily proven or disproven.

A good deal of attention in any effort to raise the level of civility in our profession must be devoted to the simple task of increasing the vocabulary of law students and lawyers. I have a strong suspicion that the perceived decline in civility is simply a decline in the typical lawyer's arsenal of insults. As motion picture and television scriptwriters increasingly resort to four-letter words for emphasis, the "dumbing down" phenomenon has infected our diatribes as well as our polite discourse. This phenomenon is comparable to that noted by Justice Robert Gardner in bemoaning the crudeness of the demands currently utilized by American robbers:

> It is a sad commentary on contemporary culture to compare "Don't say a word, don't say a mother-fucking word," with "Stand and deliver," the famous salutation of Dick Turpin and other English highwaymen. It is true that both salutations lead to robbery. However, there is a certain rich style to "Stand and deliver." . . . The speech of contemporary criminal culture has always been a rich source

GERALD F. UELMEN

of color and vitality to any language. Yet, when one compares the "bawds," "strumpets," "trulls," "cut-purses," "knaves" and "rascals" of Fielding and Smollett to the "hookers," "pimps," "Narcs," "junkies" and "snitches" of today's criminal argot, one wonders just which direction we are traveling civilization's ladder.

Justice Gardner's lament is equally applicable to the argot of attorneys. Compare calling the judge a "butt brain" to calling the judge a "mumpsimus" or a "sophronist." Compare calling opposing counsel a "jerk" with calling opposing counsel a "bigendian," a "cunctator," or a "malapert." Instead of labeling your client a "deadbeat," imagine referring to him as "embusque." Rather than calling a witness a "dirty liar," think how memorable your closing argument would be if you called him a "Vicar of Bray." A "Vicar of Bray" is a colorful British phrase describing someone whose version of the truth depends completely on who is winning. The vicar's flexibility, which allowed him to survive King Henry VIII and each of his children, is immortalized in a brief poem:

> And this is the law I will maintain until my dying day, Sir,
> That whatsoever King shall reign, I'll still be the Vicar of Bray, Sir.

A classic source of "words to describe life's indescribable people" is Dimboxes, Epopts, and Other Quidams by David Grambs (1986). Grambs offers at least ten labels that might be appropriate for judges who occupy the bench at every level:

AGELAST: One who never laughs or smiles; a total deadpan. In Yiddish, a farbissener.
BATTOLOGIST: One who repeats the same thing over and over, like a broken record, e.g., "objection overruled."
CATAGELOPHOBE: One who bristles at the least suggestion of criticism. "May the record reflect that Your Honor is bristling?"
LATITUDINARIAN: One who is broadminded, willing to stretch things a little. Now that "liberal" has become a dirty word, latitudinarian makes a nice substitute. At least it will never be reduced to four letters.

MUMPSIMUS: One who stubbornly persists in error, even after it is rationally and patiently explained. A play on sumpsimus, the stickler for precise correctness. A sumpsimus is a mumpsimus who's right.

MISOLOGIST: Hates rational discussion. You have to reduce your argument to gut level or below.

OPSIMATH: One who learns late in life. It is better that wisdom come late than that it come not at all.

PRETERIST: One who lives totally in the past. Still cites Warren Court precedents.

SOPHRONIST: One who is excessively cautious, wary, and hesitant. "Can you supply points and authorities on that relevancy objection?"

WITWANTON: One who tries to be cleverly amusing, but misses the mark.

Grambs's collection also includes ten gems that match most lists of the top ten lawyers you love to hate:

ATELOPHOBE: The morbid perfectionist. Ten pages of deposition testimony can be devoted to one typographical error.

BIG-ENDIAN: The anal-retentive with a magnifying glass. The trivial achieves epic proportions. (From Gulliver's Travels)

CACOEPIST: Consistently mispronounces words. The Cacographer consistently misspells them.

CUNCTATOR: The ultimate procrastinator. Never does anything that can be put off.

ERGOTIST: The pedantic reasoner. Every other word is "consequently" or "therefore." Not to be confused with the ERGOPHILE (workaholic) or the ERGOPHOBE (afraid of work).

MALAPERT: Impudent, always sassing back.

PRONEUR: Constant flatterer, a toady who offers nothing but praise. In Yiddish, a Tochis Lecher.

QUODLIBETARIAN: The hair-splitter who loves to divide everything into six categories, even the luncheon check.

SNOLLYGOSTER: Totally unprincipled. Keep your hand on your wallet.

ULTRACREPEDARIAN The over-reacher, whose analysis extends far beyond his own comprehension.

Below are nine ways to call a witness a liar, most drawn from Grambs:

DENTILOQUIST: Speaks through clenched teeth, with real determination.

CHIROSOPHIST: Sleight of hand artist who changes the facts faster than the court reporter can get it down.

GANSER'S SYNDROME: Compulsive inability to give a precise answer. Every answer is preceded by "about" or "approximately."

GREMIAL: The bosom friend through thick or thin. Always good for an alibi.

GRINAGOG: Always smiles even when lying. Opposite of the lachrymist, who cries on cue.

HYDRA: Grows two heads for each one you cut off. When you catch Hydra in a lie, you'll get two more in the explanation.

PHILALETHE: Loves to forget. Favorite answer is "I don't recall."

PSEUDOLOGIST: The truly systematic liar who constructs an elaborate house of cards.

SYNTONE: Goes with the flow. Will agree with contradictory propositions as long as they're advanced by two different lawyers.

We should also devote some time in any respectable civility course to a cross-cultural perspective. I personally think students would gain a great deal by learning the rudiments of Yiddish. A single Yiddish word can capture all the subtle nuances one might need to contemptuously characterize the depths to which an opposing lawyer has sunk. Rather than an indignant objection that "Counsel is deliberately interposing frivolous objections to delay these proceedings," you can simply chortle, "The nebbish is putzing up this case."

One of the great advantages of Yiddish is that the same word can be used to insult in one context and express admiration in another. *Chachem* can denote a savant of great wisdom or a foolish jerk, depending on the intonation. Thus, you might greet a judge's overruling of your objection by sighing, "Such a *chacham*."

Judges have even been known to use Yiddish labels to insult each other all the while denying that an insult was intended. In one notable California Court of Appeals opinion, a justice responded to a dissent with a footnote in which the first letter of each sentence spelled "SCHMUCK." The German definition of "schmuck" is a jewel. The

Yiddish definition is somewhat less flattering, although equally treasured by some. It refers to the male reproductive organ. The dissenter protested that English dictionaries use the Yiddish definition, and California law requires that appellate opinions be written in English. The author of the offending footnote, however, included a reference to a German dictionary. Thus, the dexterity of Yiddish insults should be apparent.

Many law schools have already incorporated some basic Yiddish into their curriculum. Justice William O. Douglas, for example, reported that the most important distinction impressed upon him as a student at Columbia Law School was the difference between a "schnook" and a "schlemiel." He said a "schnook" is a fellow who gets dressed up in his dinner jacket and goes to a very elegant dinner party and proceeds to spill the soup and then the gravy from the entree and then slobbers the chocolate sauce when dessert is served. The "schlemiel" is the person sitting next to him, upon whom he spills it. Edward Bennett Williams observed that in every case involving multiple defendants represented by separate lawyers, there is always one lawyer who's a schnook, and he makes all the other lawyers look like schlemiels.

Lest we feel too sorry for the schlemiel, however, we should note the difference between a "schlemiel," who brings on his own misfortune, and the "schlimazel," who is simply plagued by bad luck. When a schlimazel drops a piece of toast, it always lands with the butter side down. When a schlemiel drops a piece of toast, it's only after he has put butter on both sides.

Now that we have a syllabus for our course in civility, the problem is finding a professor to teach it. The traditional Socratic technique, which is undoubtedly the least civil form of dialogue ever devised, will have to be discarded. The teacher will have to serve as a role model of gracious civility. Judging from the civility of their behavior at faculty meetings, most deans will have great difficulty filling this position from their current full-time faculty. They will have to embark on a search to recruit a professor of civility.

Finding a role model of civility in today's bench and bar may require an arduous search. Even among the ranks of the justices of the U.S. Supreme Court, I'm informed, oral arguments have become embarrassing displays of sniping and snarling. Ultimately, we may have to employ the services of the Walt Disney Company to create a professor somewhat like the mechanical Abraham Lincoln at Disneyland. Perhaps

GERALD F. UELMEN

we could construct a plastic mechanical replica of John W. Davis to teach the course.

Devising a final examination for this course should be quite simple. The most efficient way to test a student's civility is a multiple-choice exam, similar to the format utilized for the Multistate Professional Responsibility Examination. A sample of twelve questions, utilizing the "quadruple distractor" format highly favored by the National Conference of Bar Examiners, follows. Under the "quadruple distractor" format, no answer is correct. The student is challenged to select the answer that is least incorrect.

The greatest challenge we will face as legal educators in the decade ahead will be to preserve the great traditions of insult and invective that have always characterized our profession while still training our students to deliver their insult and invective in a civil way. Law school courses in civility should be designed with this goal in mind.

Final Examination in Civility

1. The proper way to address Chief Justice Roberts during oral argument is:
   a. John
   b. Chief
   c. Your Excellency
   d. Most Honorable and Exalted Lordship, Sir (while drooling)

2. The proper attire for male attorneys to appear in municipal court is:
   a. Slacks and a sport shirt
   b. An Italian silk suit and alligator shoes
   c. Striped slacks and a swallowtail coat
   d. A Columbo raincoat

3. At a state dinner, U.S. Court of Appeals judges should be seated:
   a. After U.S. Supreme Court justices and before five-star generals
   b. Between five- and four-star generals
   c. Between four- and three-star generals
   d. In the kitchen

4. An "aperitif" is:
   a. A vicious breed of dog
   b. The hot towel served on some airlines to wash your hands and face
   c. Two cigars
   d. A partial denture

5. When setting the table for a Bar Association dinner, the napkin should go:
   a. Under the knife, on the left
   b. Under the knife, on the right
   c. In the water glass
   d. Draped over the back of the chair

6. In addressing a letter to a U.S. Magistrate, the appropriate salutation is:
   a. Dear Magistrate:
   b. Dear U.S.:
   c. Greetings!
   d. To Whom it May Concern:

7. When denouncing a judge's adverse ruling at a press conference, it is appropriate for a lawyer to refer to:
   a. The judge's difficulty in passing the bar exam
   b. The judge's ABA "unqualified" rating
   c. The judge's drunk driving conviction
   d. The judge's law school grades

8. Two days before a long-scheduled deposition of your client, opposing counsel calls to request a continuance, informing you his mother passed away and the funeral is set for the evening of the day of the deposition. The most appropriate response is:
   a. Can you supply a notarized death certificate?
   b. Were you close to her?
   c. Can't you get someone to substitute for you (at the funeral)?
   d. No problem. We'll finish the depo by 5:00 p.m.

GERALD F. UELMEN

9. When opposing counsel is a woman, a male attorney should address her:
   a. Miz (emphasize *zzz* with slight hiss)
   b. Madam (or Ma'am)
   c. By her first name
   d. Don't address her directly; direct all comments at the wall or the ceiling.

10. Upon receiving contributions from lawyers for his reelection campaign, a judge should:
   a. Not acknowledge receipt
   b. Send a personal note of thanks
   c. Call and pledge undying gratitude
   d. Any or all the above, depending on the amount

11. When a filing clerk refuses to accept a brief because the cover is the wrong color, you should:
   a. Berate the clerk with colorful epithets
   b. File a writ of scire facias
   c. Demand to see the chief judge immediately
   d. Offer the clerk your tickets to the twi-night doubleheader

12. When you write a nasty letter to opposing counsel, complaining that her secretary disconnected you while you were on "hold," you should:
   a. Send a copy to her client
   b. Send a copy to the judge
   c. Send a copy to the Bar Discipline Committee
   d. Send a copy to the Committee on Civility of the Seventh Federal Judicial Circuit.

---

* From *"Id.," Brigham Young University Law Review*, p. 337 (1992). The footnote to the title reads:

> This article may simply be cited "Id.," followed by a page number which need not relate to any of the page numbers in this article. No reference to the author or this law journal is necessary. We will get all the glory we need in the Guinness Book of World Records, where this article will be enshrined as the most frequently cited law review article ever written.

5

Ruminations on the Current State of Legal Education

I WAS LUCKY. My career in legal education coincided with a "golden age," in which an abundance of applicants ensured that nearly every law school could fill its seats with students who were eager to learn and had the smarts to succeed. Two factors contributed to the demise of this "golden age."

First, law schools were forced to furiously compete for the best students by the popularity of "rankings" compiled by U.S. New & World Report and its competitors. The factors that affected the rankings took over the decisions of how to allocate budgets, and many law schools became saddled with bulking faculties and staffs that required dramatic annual increases in tuition. In filling faculty positions, every law school was looking for the same thing: a scholar who was more interested in "shaping the law" through research and writing than he or she was interested in training competent practitioners. Thus, law school tuition finances a huge glut of law reviews of questionable value, being filled by professors who measure their success by the number of articles they publish. Meanwhile, students are accumulating huge debts by taking out loans to cover their tuition. By the time they earn their JD and are ready to take the bar exam, it is not uncommon for law graduates to have accumulated $100,000 to $200,000 in debt. The need to service that debt forecloses pursuing the lower-paying jobs serving the public, which motivated many of them to come to law school in the first place.

Second, overproduction of law graduates soon outpaced the employment opportunities available, at least the high-paying opportunities that many applicants seem to set their sights on. As word spread that a JD degree and admission to the bar were no guarantee of gainful employment, the pool of applicants shrunk in half.

As my retirement nears, I find little consolation in my wife's comments that "I'm getting out just in time." I occasionally feel like a rat fleeing a sinking ship. But there's no reason legal education should be immune from the economic laws of supply and demand, the same as every other endeavor. Hopefully, what will emerge are law schools that are no longer striving to all look the same, namely like Harvard or Yale. The elitism that pervades legal education from top to bottom, with everyone a rung higher in the U.S. News rankings looking down their nose at those a rung lower on the ladder, may never be eradicated. But the realization that the market for lawyer's talents is incredibly diverse will require law schools to recognize that they cannot afford to be all things to all applicants and must find a niche in which they can partner with the needs of a discrete portion of the bar.

V

The Death Penalty

1

Catholics and the Death Penalty*

S HOULD THE RELIGIOUS faith of jurors affect their reasoning on whether a defendant should be executed? Another way to ask this question is to inquire whether jurors should "compartmentalize" their religious or moral views and attempt to ignore them in reaching their decision. Although I think former president Bill Clinton deserves the heavyweight title for being the "Great Compartmentalizer" when it comes to morals, Justice Antonin Scalia certainly comes a close second. He describes his role as a justice of the Supreme Court as follows:

> I try mightily to prevent my religious views or my political views or my philosophical views from affecting my interpretation of the laws, which is what my job is about. I read texts. I'm always reading a text and trying to give it the fairest interpretation possible. That's all I do. How can my religious views have anything to do with that? They can make me leave the bench if I find that I'm enmeshed in an immoral operation, but the only one of my religious views that has anything to do with my job as a judge is the seventh commandment—thou shalt not lie. I try to observe that faithfully, but other than that I don't think any of my religious views have anything to do with how I do my job as a judge.

Clearly, the role assigned to a juror in our system is very different from the role assigned to a justice of the Supreme Court. A Supreme Court justice interprets the meaning of the Constitution and statutes but does not engage in the kind of normative determination jurors are expected to make in a death penalty case. Here is how the jurors' task is described in the instructions given to the jury in every death penalty case tried in California:

> The weighing of aggravating and mitigating circumstances does not mean a mere mechanical counting of factors on each side of an imaginary scale, or the arbitrary assignment of weights to any of them. You are free to assign whatever moral or sympathetic value you deem appropriate to each and all of the various factors you are permitted to consider. In weighing the various circumstances you determine under the relevant evidence which penalty is justified and appropriate by considering the totality of the aggravating circumstances with the totality of the mitigating circumstances. To return a judgment of death, each of you must be persuaded that the aggravating circumstances are so substantial in comparison with the mitigating circumstances that it warrants death instead of life without parole.

Justice Scalia suggests that jurors deliberating the death penalty should compartmentalize and ignore their religious beliefs, as should governors in reviewing clemency petitions:

> [I]f I were in that position as either a juror or a governor I wouldn't feel free to act upon my own religious beliefs. I'm there representing the community. If I were a governor, as to whether I should commute a sentence, I would want standards. I would say it seems to me the sentence ought to be commuted if these factors exist, but not because I'm a bleeding-heart Christian. That ought to have nothing to do with it.

While Justice Scalia's point may have limited relevance to a governor considering a pardon application, it is an inaccurate characterization of the juror's role, at least in a death penalty case. While jurors are drawn from a cross section of the community, they are not put in the jury box to "represent" anyone. They have no constituency and are not answerable to the "community" for how they vote. As Judge Learned Hand famously observed, "The individual can forfeit his liberty—to say nothing of his life—only at the hands of those who, unlike any official, are in no wise accountable, directly or indirectly, for what they do, and who at once separate and melt anonymously in the community from which they came. . . . [S]ince if they acquit their verdict is final, no one is likely to suffer of whose conduct they do not morally disapprove. . . ."

I find a striking parallel between the way that our courts deal with the injection of religion into death deliberations and the way they deal with the issue of jury nullification. Both are treated like crocodiles in the bathtub. We are constantly aware of their presence but make a studied effort to ignore them. While a jury has the undeniable power to ignore the law and acquit a defendant simply because they believe the law under which the defendant is being prosecuted is unjust, courts consistently refuse to instruct juries that they have this power and will not permit lawyers to urge juries to exercise it. Some courts have even permitted the removal of individual jurors who seem intent on exercising their power of nullification to the dismay of their fellow jurors. But jurors who consider their personal religious values in a death penalty case are not engaged in jury nullification. They are not choosing to ignore the law. They are following it. Why not tell them that by instructing them: "You may consider your personal religious, moral, and ethical values and beliefs in weighing the aggravating and mitigating factors and deciding whether death or life imprisonment is justified as the punishment in this case." Perhaps one reason defense lawyers do not request such an instruction and oppose it if it is requested by the prosecution is because they fear that more jurors will rely upon religious views that favor the death penalty. The process by which we select jurors for death penalty trials fully justifies that fear. Jurors whose religious views disfavor death are less likely to make it through the selection process than jurors whose religious views encourage its use.

There are many deeply held beliefs that may influence a Catholic juror's decision whether to impose a sentence of death, apart from the church's position on the death penalty. Belief in personal redemption for one's sins might persuade one that life without the possibility of parole is a more appropriate sentence because it provides an opportunity for redemption. Belief in a final judgment to be rendered by God might also influence a juror to exercise mercy. Additionally, acceptance of the presence of Christ in every other person—even a murderer— could have a profound impact on the choice between death and life imprisonment. Catholics who serve as jurors in death penalty cases need not "compartmentalize" and ignore such beliefs. Being a "bleeding-heart Christian" should have much to do with the way that a Catholic makes the momentous choice that our death penalty laws place in the hands and hearts of jurors.

How much does my being a Catholic have to do with my opposition to the death penalty? I started out in my legal career after eighteen years of Catholic education—four with the Carmelites, eight with the Jesuits. As a prosecutor, I had no qualms about the death penalty, although I never had to ask a jury for a death sentence. Fifteen years later, I concluded that the death penalty is unethical, immoral, and unacceptable under any circumstances. The change in my position was a direct result of fifteen years of exposure to the vagaries of the criminal justice system. I would not be a "death qualified" juror, and if I were a judge, I would have to recuse myself in a death penalty case. I reached the conclusion that the death penalty is immoral not because of anything that the pope or any bishop had to say about it, although giving respectful consideration to those views has certainly reinforced my own. I must confess that I was impressed by what Mother Teresa had to say after she came to California and visited our death row at San Quentin. After surveying the rows of cells in which we now confine more than 750 men to await a final walk to the death chamber, she poked her bony finger into the chest of the burly guard who escorted her and said, "Remember, what you do to these men, you do to God." I reached my judgment about the death penalty because I, both as a prosecutor and a defense lawyer, have seen firsthand the imperfections of our system of justice. I still believe it is the best system of justice in the world. But nevertheless, it simply cannot be trusted to reliably, fairly, and consistently sort out who should live and who should die. I think a lottery would be a better system. If we sentenced every murderer to life imprisonment and a lottery ticket and then once a year conducted the "big spin" to pick those who would be executed, we would save billions of dollars and achieve approximately the same result that our current system of appeals and habeas corpus petitions and writs of certiorari accomplish. Now is that a position based upon an ethical or moral judgment? I suppose it is. And I really cannot compartmentalize it and separate it from my religious faith. What I am really saying is that it is morally wrong for the state to take the life of a criminal, unless the state has a flawless system of justice to reliably, fairly, and consistently determine who should and who should not be executed. I believe it is simply impossible for human beings to devise a flawless

GERALD F. UELMEN

system of justice. If you reject my "big spin" as immoral, you should reject the death penalty on the same grounds of immorality. I am not advocating or suggesting that Catholics should misrepresent their views opposing capital punishment in order to get on juries and "sabotage" the administration of the death penalty. Catholics who fully agree with my views should openly express them and accept the consequences of dismissal as jurors. Catholic judges who agree with me should recuse themselves in death cases. Catholic prosecutors who agree with me should decline to accept assignments as prosecutors in death cases. As the proportion of jurors, judges, and prosecutors who refuse to participate in the continued administration of a morally bankrupt law continues to grow, more and more states will reconsider the wisdom of continuing this folly and will join with the civilized nations of the world in rejecting laws that permit death as a penalty.

---

* From "Catholic Jurors and the Death Penalty," *Journal of Catholic Legal Studies,* vol. 44, p. 355 (2005).

2

The Crocodile in the Bathtub*

THE LATE HONORABLE Otto Kaus, a good and gracious friend who served on the California Supreme Court from 1980 through 1985, used a marvelous metaphor to describe the dilemma of deciding controversial cases while facing reelection. He said it was like finding a crocodile in your bathtub when you go in to shave in the morning. You know it's there, and you try not to think about it, but it's hard to think about much else while you're shaving. In 1996, we saw two more respected and conscientious state Supreme Court justices fall victim to the crocodile's bite. Justice Penny White was appointed to the Tennessee Supreme Court in January of 1995. She participated in one death penalty decision, joining two other justices on her five-judge court in reversing a death penalty judgment in June of 1996. By unhappy coincidence, Justice White was the only supreme court justice on the ballot two months later. The governor saw an opportunity to gain another Republican seat on the court. He denounced Justice White as a judge who was soft on the death penalty and weak on victims' rights. His campaign succeeded, and she was removed from office after winning only 44.8 percent of the votes.

Justice David Lanphier was appointed to the Nebraska Supreme Court in 1993, shortly after a term limits initiative measure was adopted by Nebraska voters by a 70 percent margin. In May 1994, Justice Lanphier authored a unanimous opinion of the Nebraska Supreme Court holding the term limits initiative invalid because it had not complied with a constitutional amendment increasing the number of signatures required to qualify the measure for the ballot. The sponsors of the initiative then trained their sights on Justice Lanphier and mounted a well-financed campaign to unseat him. In November of 1996, he was removed by the voters, winning only 32 percent of the vote in a retention election. The justices of supreme courts in twenty-three states face contested elections at some stage in their career. Supreme court justices in another fifteen states face retention elections to keep their jobs. The death penalty is not the only crocodile in their bathtubs. Abortion remains a hot-button issue in many states, and final resolution of federal issues now clears the deck for state constitutional issues to be presented for the first time to many state supreme courts. And in the twenty-one states that allow legislation by popular initiative, justices frequently encounter an accusation that they are thwarting the voters' will by striking down popular initiative measures. The vulnerability of state supreme court justices has also been enhanced by a number of "megatrends" in the life of modern America. The nature and extent of media coverage of judicial proceedings has changed dramatically in recent years. The tabloidization of the media, ratings-driven competition in more diverse media markets, and the reduction of news coverage to ten-second sound bites have rendered efforts to educate the public about the judicial process largely ineffectual. The climate of political discourse has also sharply deteriorated, with partisan maneuvering and lack of civility becoming defining elements. Political lobbies and special interest groups no longer confine their persuasive efforts to the legislative process but closely follow court decisions. Supreme court justices who not so long ago quietly contemplated the polite parsing of their opinions by academic scholars now encounter furious denunciation by special interests who, while frequently appearing as friends of the court, are often the court's worst enemies. The greatest challenge facing state supreme courts in the coming century will be the maintenance of judicial independence in an era of increasing politicization of the judicial office. I believe the biggest mistake we can make in facing this challenge is to throw it into the laps of the justices and tell them, "It's your problem." Obviously, it is a problem for every citizen devoted to the rule of law and its preservation. Most especially, it is a problem that demands a major commitment from the organized bar.

And speaking of crocodiles, we need to contemplate the lesson taught by one of the greatest philosophers ever to emerge from an American swamp. I refer, of course, to Pogo, the wise possum created by cartoonist Walt Kelly. Pogo was heard saying on a number of occasions, "We have met the enemy, and he is us." When he said that, Pogo was frequently speaking to his friend Albert. Albert was a crocodile of the alligator species who smoked cigars. Just as in the cartoon, we can't kill the crocodile. The crocodile is not an alien invader, but a manifestation of the public that our courts serve. The question for us to contemplate is, how can one serve the crocodile without becoming its meal? Let me take you through the swamp. We may find there are valuable lessons to be learned from some of our encounters with crocodiles during the past ten years.

The American appetite for the death penalty is best reflected in one stark statistic. There are more than three thousand men and women on death rows across the country. At the close of 1996, California led the parade with 420, Texas had 404, Florida was at 362, and Pennsylvania was in fourth place with 196. The supreme courts of these and other states find that the processing of death penalty appeals and petitions for postconviction relief consumes a bigger slice of the docket each succeeding year. To get a quick estimate, I counted up the total number of published opinions produced by the supreme courts of six death penalty states for 1985 and again for 1995, the most recent year for which data is available. I then ascertained what proportion of these opinions were death penalty cases. The six states selected were California, Illinois, Indiana, Ohio, Texas, and Virginia. It's interesting that the total number of published opinions produced by these courts actually declined 13.5 percent during the ten-year interval ending in 1995. Like the U.S. Supreme Court, state supreme courts are becoming more selective in filling their dockets, and they are deciding fewer cases. But there is one portion of their docket that these courts have little control over: the automatic appeals of death penalty judgments. The number of death penalty cases decided by these six courts increased 31 percent between 1985 and 1995. In 1985, 5.5 percent of the published opinions produced by these six courts were in death cases. In 1995, that proportion increased to 8.3 percent. The number of published opinions, of course, is a rather crude measure of the proportion of a state supreme court justice's workload devoted to death penalty review. Many justices in these states would agree with the estimate of recently retired California Chief Justice Malcolm Lucas, who told me death cases are now 20 to 25 percent of the workload of the California Supreme Court. What may be most disconcerting about the death penalty cases during the past ten years, however, is the increase in the rate of affirmance by some state supreme courts. Ten years ago, these six supreme courts affirmed 63 percent of the death penalty judgments they reviewed.

GERALD F. UELMEN

In 1995, 90 percent of the death penalty judgments reviewed were affirmed. While California accounts for a disproportionate share of this sample, going from an affirmance rate of zero in 1985 to a rate of 94 percent in 1995, the affirmance rate in Texas went from 86 percent to 96 percent during the same ten-year period.

While some of this increase may be attributable to the law becoming more settled, I don't believe it can be denied that some of the increase is attributable to the presence of the crocodile in the bathtub. There are disturbing indications that judicial reluctance to reverse death penalty judgments may sometimes be reluctance to expose one's posterior to the wrath of the electorate. Crocodiles do occasionally bite. In California, as we well know, three justices were removed from the state supreme court in the purge of 1986. The campaign that unseated them featured campaign ads promising that "no" votes against the retention of these three justices were the equivalent of three "yes" votes for the death penalty. Apparently, we set a standard for judicial politicking that has been emulated beyond our borders. Supreme court elections in at least ten states have been dominated by death penalty politicking in the past decade, and California and Tennessee are not the only states to see incumbent justices removed. Two justices were removed from the Mississippi Supreme Court after two separate campaigns focusing on death penalty issues. Justice James Robertson was defeated in 1992 after he was attacked for two dissenting opinions in death penalty affirmances. Ironically, when both cases were reviewed by the U.S. Supreme Court, the majority agreed with Justice Robertson's dissents and reversed the convictions. In 1990, Mississippi Supreme Court Justice William Joel Blass was defeated by an opponent promising to be a "tough judge for tough times," who attacked the incumbent justice for being "soft on crime." In both contested elections, the challenger was endorsed by the Mississippi Prosecutors Association.

In 1992, I published the results of a study correlating death penalty affirmance rates for all state supreme courts for the ten-year period ending in 1987, with the manner of judicial selection used for the justices on those courts. The thirty-eight states that then had a death penalty included states that appoint their justices for life, as in the federal system; states that utilize uncontested retention elections, such as California and Arizona; states that permit contested but nonpartisan elections, such as Georgia and Illinois; states that require judges to run under party labels, such as Texas and Mississippi; and even a handful of states where justices are elected by the legislature, such as Virginia and South Carolina. The results suggest that judges whose tenure is more secure are more willing to overturn a death penalty judgment:

Executive Appointment	26.3%
Uncontested Retention Elections	55.3%
Nonpartisan Contested Elections	62.9%
Partisan Contested Elections	62.5%
Legislative Elections	63.7%

The state that seems to have managed the death penalty crocodile with the greatest success is the state that probably has the largest indigenous population of crocodiles: Florida. The Florida Supreme Court reviewed fifty death penalty judgments in 1995 and chalked up a reversal rate of 52 percent, one of the highest reversal rates in America. Is it because the justices of the Florida Supreme Court are not subjected to the political pressures prevalent in other death penalty states? Hardly. Although Florida utilizes a retention election system in which justices face a yes-no confirmation vote every six years, recent years have, with disturbing regularity, seen organized campaigns mounted to remove targeted justices. In 1990, then chief justice Leander Shaw Jr. had to raise $300,000 for a campaign to retain his seat in the face of an organized campaign by anti-abortion forces to remove him from office. And in 1992, Justice Rosemary Barkett faced an organized campaign not only by anti-abortion forces, but also by prosecutors and police unhappy that she joined in a dissenting opinion in one controversial death penalty case, even though she had voted to affirm over two hundred death penalty appeals during her previous nine years on the court. While she won retention with 60.9 percent of the vote, the death penalty issue was trotted out in an effort to defeat her 1994 appointment to the U.S. Court of Appeals for the Eleventh Circuit, and it persuaded presidential candidate Bob Dole to place her on the list of Clinton appointees he labeled the judicial "hall of shame." How is it that Florida has managed to maintain an independent state supreme court that rigorously reviews death penalty cases, reversing between one-half and one-third of the cases it reviews every year? One might speculate that Florida has defused public frustration by the delivery of actual executions. Florida has successfully executed thirty-eight inmates since 1978, and the Florida Supreme Court has maintained a brisk pace of appellate review, deciding as many as seventy-three death penalty appeals in a single year. Perhaps the public frustration so frequently misdirected at courts is really frustration with the total lack of executions rather than with reversals in particular cases. California in 1986 and Tennessee in 1996 had yet to see their death penalty law ever enforced. I'm not proposing it as a solution, but one reality we may have to face is that this crocodile must be occasionally fed; if he isn't, he will eat his keepers. That explanation, however, is hard to reconcile with the fact that Texas has delivered 107 executions since 1978, and the pace of review by the Texas Court of Criminal Appeals is close to that of Florida.

Why would such a fat, well-fed crocodile turn on its keeper? It may simply be that Texas crocodiles grow bigger and hungrier than anywhere else, and we shouldn't try to learn anything from the Texas experience. Two years ago, a young lawyer who had experienced the Texas death penalty system firsthand, as a law clerk for a judge on the U.S. Court of Appeals for the Fifth Circuit and as an attorney for the Texas Death Penalty Resource Center, left Texas to join the Capital Litigation Unit of the Florida State Public Defender's office in Miami. Writing for the *Texas Lawyer*, Brent Newton offered some interesting reflections on why the affirmance rate was so much higher in Texas than in Florida. The most significant factor he identified was "the disparate quality of appellate judges in the two states, which is largely a function of the fact that judges on the Florida Supreme Court are not elected in partisan popular elections, as are the judges on the Texas Court of Criminal Appeals." He also noted that the Florida Supreme Court reviews the weighing of aggravating and mitigating circumstances in the death penalty determination on appeal, while the Texas court refuses to consider whether a life sentence was more appropriate in view of the mitigating circumstances. Many death penalty reversals by the Florida Supreme Court come in cases where the jury actually recommended life imprisonment, but the recommendation was overridden by the trial judge. The availability of judicial override has yielded what Justice Sandra Day O'Connor recently called "ostensibly surprising statistics." Only four states allow judges to disregard a jury's recommendation on the death penalty, and the same pattern has emerged in all four states. In Alabama, trial judges override jury recommendations of life and impose a death sentence almost ten times as frequently as they override recommendations of death. In Florida, trial judges overrode jury recommendations in 185 cases between 1972 and 1992. In 134 of these, trial judges opted for death over a life recommendation of the jury. In Indiana, the ratio was eight judicial overrides for death to four for life between 1980 and 1994. Why are trial judges more likely than jurors to favor executions? Justice John Paul Stevens put his finger on the problem in a dissenting opinion to the U.S. Supreme Court ruling upholding the Alabama provisions for judicial override in death penalty cases:

> The "higher authority" to whom present-day capital judges may be "too responsive" is a political climate in which judges who covet higher office—or who merely wish to remain judges—must constantly profess their fealty to the death penalty. . . . The danger that they will bend to political pressures when pronouncing sentence in highly publicized capital cases is the same danger confronted by judges beholden to King George.

Seen in this light, the high reversal rate in Florida may to some extent be a corrective for the politicization of death penalty decisions by judicial override in the trial courts. While Florida Supreme Court justices are also subject to the same political pressures, they are at least insulated by the device of yes-no retention elections, unlike the contested elections faced by trial judges in Florida and by judges of the Texas Court of Criminal Appeals. In the 1996 elections, three justices of the Florida Supreme Court were retained with no opposition. But retention elections are not always protection from the crocodile. Ask Justice Penny White of Tennessee or Justice David Lanphier of Nebraska or Chief Justice Rose Bird and Associate Justices Joseph Grodin and Cruz Reynoso of California. All of them lost their seats in retention elections. It cannot be denied, however, that the crocodile is more voracious in states that have contested elections. Judges who vote to affirm in every death penalty case will be the first to loudly proclaim that the public pressure of electoral politics is not a problem. No judge would ever admit that his or her vote was influenced by public pressure or popular opinion. It takes a truly sensitive judge to even engage in the soul-searching inquiry into the impact of the crocodiles in the bathtub upon his or her decision-making process. Since most death penalty trials involve lengthy proceedings with complex evidentiary issues, there will be errors or failures of counsel to be found in many of the records reviewed. An affirmance is easily rationalized by the harmless error rule or by a relaxed standard of competence for lawyers. Opinions that affirm are rarely scrutinized or criticized by the press, and when they are, the criticism can be deflected or ignored by attributing it to "liberals" who are opposed to the death penalty. Probably the most insidious influence of the death penalty crocodile is on the quality of counsel in death cases. Judges who owe their election to a campaign commitment to enforcing the death penalty will be more likely to countenance lazy and sloppy lawyers. When one compares the published opinions in death penalty opinions issued by the Florida Supreme Court with those of the Texas Court of Criminal Appeals, one encounters a profound difference in attitude regarding the degree of competency to be demanded of court-appointed defense counsel. Brent Newton sums it up as follows:

> Horror stories regarding Texas capital defense lawyers—*e.g.*, lawyers who engage in little or no preparation for trial, lawyers who were drunk or fell asleep at trial, openly racist lawyers representing minority clients—are legion. Unlike the state and federal appellate courts in Florida, appellate judges in Texas are generally willing to turn a blind eye to such shameful lawyering.

Regretfully, his observation of Texas courts is occasionally applicable to California. Too often, the lawyers who are criticized by judges are not the lawyers who slept through trials or did too little to prepare their client's defense. Instead, judicial wrath is visited upon the lawyers who do "too much" for their clients by vigorously asserting every conceivable ground for reversal. Part of the problem with the review of death penalty judgments by state supreme courts today is that the siege mentality afflicting the justices leads them to regard the defense bar as the enemy. In California, our supreme court watched quietly as the governor dismantled the state public defender's office, and then the court itself trashed the appellate project created to fill the void. Largely as a result, over 140 of the occupants of California's death row are not yet represented by appellate counsel. A recent study by the Texas Bar Foundation concludes that Texas also faces a crisis in providing competent counsel for death penalty appeals and postconviction proceedings. The establishment of public defender offices has been fiercely resisted in Texas, while the Texas Court of Criminal Appeals still debates whether *Gideon v. Wainwright* was correctly decided.

The organized bar should be the loudest defender of judicial independence. When special interest groups or victims' rights organizations suggest that their unhappiness with a particular decision should result in the removal of the judges who rendered it, the judges are hardly in a position to respond with a spirited defense of judicial integrity and independence. Too often, the response is simply silence, which reinforces the impression that judicial elections can become referendums on the popularity of particular decisions. When that agenda is endorsed by elected political leaders at the highest level, courts are left in a highly vulnerable position that truly threatens the principle of judicial independence. Yet when it is appropriate for a court to speak out in defense of the principle that indigent death row inmates should be competently represented, the judicial silence is often deafening. Last October, when Congress cut off funding for the twenty death penalty resource centers engaged in raising the level of competence of defense lawyers in death cases, how many state supreme courts did Congress hear from?

Our travels through the swamp with Pogo may offer some tentative lessons about how we can preserve and protect the vulnerable tadpole of judicial independence. One of my favorite Pogo adventures was the crisis he encountered when asked by a friendly mama frog to babysit her tadpole. The tadpole was swimming in a mason jar that Albert "mistook" for a martini with an olive. Pogo was ready to climb down Albert's throat himself to retrieve the victim but was dissuaded when Albert insisted on a farewell handshake. Pogo then came up with a brilliant solution: he made Albert drink so much water that the tadpole was able to swim back out to Pogo's arms. Pogo then declares that the solution is "not so hard once we puts our minds to it." Once we "puts our minds to it," the problem of preserving judicial independence in an era of judicial politicization becomes a question of political will. Do those who value the independence of the judiciary have the will to fight for it in the political arena? Do they value it enough to put it ahead of their political agenda of gaining "control" of a court for a political party or a special interest? Do they value it enough to finance the campaigns that will have to be mounted on behalf of judges who are targeted for defeat because of the unpopularity of their decisions?

The answers to these questions are by no means obvious. We cannot assume that all lawyers or even all judges are strongly committed to the principle of judicial independence. We have recently witnessed the spectacle of candidates for the presidency of the United States and governorships of our largest states calling for the resignation or the defeat of judges because they didn't like the decisions they rendered. If lawyers, who should know better, are more committed to gaining personal political advantage than to preserving the principle of judicial independence, how will we ever convince the electorate they should look beyond their disagreements with a particular decision? There are many potential reforms that could make judges less vulnerable, even if the principle of electoral accountability is preserved. Contested elections, especially partisan ones, have little to recommend themselves. While retention elections are no guarantee of independence, they are certainly an improvement over contested elections. The timing of judicial elections should also be examined. In California, we only vote on the retention of supreme court justices in gubernatorial years, thus increasing the risk that judicial retention could be politicized as an issue in the governor's race. Giving judges longer terms is another reform that would enhance their independence and put some distance between a controversial decision and an election. Many advocates of judicial independence stress the importance of "educating the public" about what judges do and why their independence should be valued. It has even been suggested that the normal rule that judges don't publicly discuss or debate the reasoning for their decisions should be suspended when judges face an election contest. There are others who point out that public understanding of what courts do doesn't necessarily increase public support for the courts. Perhaps judicial survival is enhanced by judicial invisibility. I find it hard to imagine how even the most reticent judges can avoid controversy, however, when they must decide the kinds of issues that regularly come before the supreme court of every state. The reality is that every justice who faces an election contest to keep his or her job is a tadpole in a pond full of crocodiles.

---

* From "Crocodiles in the Bathtub: Maintaining the Independence of State Supreme Courts in an Era of Judicial Politicization," *Notre Dame Law Review,* vol. 72, p. 1133 (1997).

3

California's Dysfunctional Death Penalty*

IN 2004, I was appointed to serve as executive director for the California Commission on the Fair Administration of Justice, created by the California Senate Rules Committee. At the time, I did not realize I was being invited to a wake. Although the commission was remarkably successful in achieving consensus to fulfill its charge—to make recommendations designed to ensure that the application of criminal justice in California is just, fair, and accurate—and was remarkably successful in marshaling seven of its proposals through the California legislature, every one of those proposals was then vetoed by California governor Arnold Schwarzenegger! We learned that having law enforcement participation on the commission and having unanimous commission support for our recommendations did not guarantee law enforcement support when these measures landed on the governor's desk. And our then governor was apparently more impressed by the opposition of the California Police Chiefs Association and the California State Sheriffs' Association than by the recommendations of our commission. Although this was a frustrating experience, I fully realized that criminal law reform is not a sport for the short-winded. I was confident that the election of a new governor would lead to full implementation of our commission's proposals to improve eyewitness identification procedures, require the recording of police interrogations, require the corroboration of jail snitch testimony, improve standards for forensic science, require the reporting of prosecutorial misconduct to the state bar, and support the reintegration of the exonerated innocent into society. Most of these reforms have since been enacted and signed by Governor Jerry Brown, who was a member of the commission while serving as attorney general.

I was less optimistic about the effect of our report on the administration of California's death penalty law. The reform of California's death penalty law will take more than the election of a new governor. Our death penalty law was adopted by initiative, and in California, an initiative measure can be amended only by a subsequent initiative. Thus, death penalty reform will require a vote of the people, and the level of popular support for the death penalty in California remained at 63 percent at the time our report was released in 2008. Since then, support for the death penalty has dramatically dropped. In 2012, 48 percent of the California electorate supported an initiative to abolish capital punishment in California. Despite spending more than any other state on its implementation and administration, California today is saddled with a death penalty law that can be described only as completely dysfunctional. We have the longest death row in America, with approximately 750 inmates awaiting execution. Typically, the lapse of time between sentence and execution is twenty-five years, twice the national average, and is growing wider each year. A total of 119 inmates have spent more than twenty years on California's death row. Most of them will certainly die before they are ever executed. Since restoration of the death penalty in 1978, the leading cause of death on California's death row has been death by natural causes (thirty-eight), followed by suicides (fourteen), and executions (thirteen). For all practical purposes, a sentence of death in California is a sentence of life imprisonment without the possibility of parole. The only difference is that the individual serves the life sentence on death row while the state forks out millions of dollars to process appeals and habeas corpus proceedings. Additionally, the cost of confinement is quadruple what it would be if the individual was serving the life sentence in a maximum security prison, where those sentenced to life imprisonment normally serve their sentences. How did we create this mess?

In constructing our machinery of death, we took four steps in California that inexorably led us into our current morass. First, we enacted the broadest death penalty law in America, with an array of special circumstances that can be applied to 87 percent of the murders committed in California. There is nothing "special" about special circumstances under California's death penalty law. Special circumstances, for example, include murders perpetrated in the commission of twelve different felonies, regardless of whether the defendant was the person who actually perpetrated the murder.

Second, we gave fifty-eight locally elected county prosecutors complete discretion to determine which murders should be prosecuted as death penalty cases. Our commission discovered tremendous disparity among the various counties in California in the degree to which the death penalty was utilized. In San Francisco, two successive district attorneys have been elected on a pledge that they will never employ the death penalty. In more rural counties, district attorneys are regularly elected and reelected on a pledge they will employ the death penalty as frequently as possible. As a result, the numbers of new death judgments in California soon escalated beyond the capacity of courts to keep up. For the twenty years between 1980 and 2000, California averaged thirty-two new death judgments each year.

Third, we enshrined this statutory scheme in an initiative measure, which rendered it virtually impossible to narrow the application of the law by legislative amendment.

Fourth, we purged our state supreme court of justices who attempted to narrow the application of California's death penalty. From 1978 until 1986, the California Supreme Court under Chief Justice Rose Bird affirmed only 8 percent of the death judgments it reviewed, imposing stringent requirements upon the jury instructions to be given in felony murder special circumstance cases. In the November election of 1986, California voters removed Chief Justice Bird and Associate Justices Cruz Reynoso and Joseph Grodin from office, largely on the campaign claim that votes against these three would be three votes in favor of the death penalty. The election results had a profound effect upon their successors. From 1986 to 1996, the California Supreme Court under Chief Justice Malcolm Lucas affirmed 94 percent of the death judgments it reviewed.

After a comprehensive review of the costs and benefits of the death penalty, the New Jersey Death Penalty Commission concluded that there is no compelling evidence that the death penalty rationally serves a legitimate penological intent, that the costs of the death penalty are greater than the costs of life in prison without parole, that the penological interest in executing a small number of persons is not sufficiently compelling to justify the risk of making an irreversible mistake, and that the alternative of life imprisonment in a maximum security institution without the possibility of parole would sufficiently ensure public safety and address other legitimate social and penological interests, including the interests of the families of murder victims. These considerations led the State of New Jersey to abolish the death penalty in 2007 in favor of the alternative of life imprisonment without parole (LWOP). A similar step was taken by the State of New Mexico in 2008 for the same reasons. The same alternative is available in California, although this step would have to be approved by the voters. California has had a sentence of life imprisonment without possibility of parole available since 1978. According to the California Department of Corrections, 3,622 defendants were serving LWOP sentences as of January 1, 2008, including some who were initially charged in death penalty cases. Thus, throughout the past thirty years, we have increased our LWOP population at an average rate of 120 defendants per year. If the death penalty were replaced with LWOP sentences, not only would the costs of confinement be significantly reduced, but many of the costs of trial and appellate review for death cases would be eliminated as well.

At the trial level, substantial savings would result from the elimination of the necessity for death-qualified juries. In Los Angeles County, eight hundred potential jurors may be summoned for a death penalty case. California jury commissioners rely solely upon voter registration and Department of Motor Vehicles lists to summon jurors, although state law permits expansion of source lists. Because of the length of the trial, 75 percent of potential jurors will be excused for financial hardship. California courts pay jurors at a rate of $15 per day. Many employers do not pay employees for jury service, and those who do frequently limit the payment to no more than two weeks. The remaining jurors must undergo individual questioning to determine whether they have opinions about the death penalty that would preclude their serving in a death case. This process of "death qualification" has resulted in larger numbers of potential jurors being excused as public opinion against the death penalty has grown. While a jury is normally selected in one or two days in most felony cases, the selection of a death-qualified jury normally takes eight to ten days of court time. The use of limited source lists, the exclusion of a higher proportion of potential jurors for economic hardship, and the exclusion of those who disapprove of the death penalty result in juries that do not reflect a cross section of the community to the extent that nondeath juries do.

Upon conviction of first-degree murder and a finding of at least one special circumstance, the same jury is required to return for a second trial, the penalty phase in which the jury decides between a sentence of death or a sentence of life imprisonment without possibility of parole. This is a full trial, with opening statements, presentation of evidence by both sides, closing arguments, and jury instructions. The jury is asked to weigh aggravating and mitigating circumstances and impose a sentence of death if aggravating circumstances outweigh mitigating circumstances or a sentence of life imprisonment without possibility of parole if mitigating circumstances outweigh aggravating circumstances. The jury must unanimously agree as to the penalty; if the jurors are unable to achieve unanimity, another jury must be impaneled to decide the penalty.

The expenses for trial and appellate counsel would also be substantially reduced if lifetime incarceration became the maximum penalty in California. Only one defense lawyer would have to be appointed for the trial. There would be no automatic appeal to the California Supreme Court, so appeals would be handled much more expeditiously by the courts of appeal. Between June 2005 and June 2006, the California Courts of Appeal decided one hundred LWOP appeals after an average delay of 18.6 months. While habeas corpus petitions are available, there is no right to appointed counsel as there is for appeals and for habeas petitions in death cases. And because there is no discretion in the exercise of the sentencing function, there is no issue regarding the adequacy of investigation of mitigating evidence or the effective assistance of counsel at a sentencing trial. Finally, although the risks of wrongful convictions remain, there would be no wrongful executions. New trials could be ordered if necessary, and the exonerated would be released.

If the New Jersey / New Mexico approach were used in California, the death penalty backlog would immediately disappear. The issues being litigated in direct appeals and habeas petitions would no longer have to be decided by the California Supreme Court. Penalty issues would not have to be decided at all. Forty death penalty trials each year would simply be added to the existing schedule of LWOP cases; instead of 120 LWOP cases per year, there would be 160. With a dysfunctional death penalty law, the reality is that most California death sentences are actually sentences of lifetime incarceration anyway. The defendant is more likely to die in prison rather than by execution. The same result can be achieved at a savings of well over $100 million by sentencing the defendant to lifetime incarceration without possibility of parole.

The current system is also unfair to defendants with plausible claims of prejudicial error in their trials or sentencing proceedings. Of the fifty-four California death cases that have been resolved with finality in the federal courts, thirty-eight of them, or 70 percent, have resulted in the grant of some relief despite the rulings of the California Supreme Court upholding the convictions and sentences. Twenty-four of them have been sent back to the California courts for penalty retrials, to be followed by another round of direct appeal and habeas proceedings. Fourteen of them had their underlying convictions set aside. The delays in reaching these conclusions often impose serious prejudice upon the defendant. No one wins when a state's dispensation of justice becomes dysfunctional. Respect for the justice system is only diminished. Then California chief justice Ronald M. George warned the California Commission on the Fair Administration of Justice that if nothing is done, the backlogs in postconviction proceedings will continue to grow "until the system falls of its own weight." The commission itself warned the legislature that doing nothing would be the worst possible course. Both warnings have gone unheeded. While some opponents of the death penalty might welcome the collapse of the machinery of death, the consequences of such a collapse would reach far beyond the fate of those on California's death row. The failure of California' s death penalty law creates cynicism and disrespect for the rule of law, produces even greater havoc in the correctional system, and undermines public respect for judges, legislators, and police.

---

*   From "Death Penalty Appeals and Habeas Proceedings: The California Experience," *Marquette Law Review,* vol. 93, p. 496 (2009–2010).

4

Ruminations on the Death Penalty

THE PARADE OF states recently repealing their death penalty laws now includes Connecticut, Maryland, and Nebraska. While that still leaves thirty-one states with a death penalty on the books, executions were actually performed in only seven states in 2014. Clearly, the trend of public opinion is moving against the death penalty. I never thought I would live to see its end in California, but I'm hopeful we can succeed with a repeal initiative in 2016.

The success of the gay marriage movement demonstrates how quickly public opinion can shift in today's Internet world. But it's easy to imagine a scenario in which it shifts the other way again. I thought we were on the verge of finally abolishing the death penalty in the 1960s and early 1970s. So did many of the justices then on the U.S. and California supreme courts. But rising homicide rates and a long run of grisly mass murders provided all the ammunition the proponents of death needed, and they very successfully used fear to manipulate public opinion. It can happen again, especially if we see an increase in terrorism in the United States. Every time some idiot shoots up an airport or a school, there will be politicians to suggest that we "need" a death penalty to deter such travesties or that the only appropriate response to such callous disregard of life is to take the lives of the perpetrators. Even in states that have abolished capital punishment, like Massachusetts, the federal death penalty can be employed as it was in the case of the Boston Marathon bomber. Abolishing the federal death penalty may be the toughest battle of all because of its successful employment in terrorist cases. While it won't have a deterrent effect to diminish the number of such tragedies, the justification of retribution is at its strongest in such cases. Once we are left with revenge or retribution as the only possible justification remaining, we come face–to-face with the moral arguments. That's what makes me uneasy. The shift in public opinion is not attributable to the success of moral arguments, but practical ones.

VI

The Drug War

The Impact of Drugs on Sentencing Policy*

I WAS RECENTLY asked who inspired me to become a criminal defense lawyer. I immediately thought of Sister Emerentia, the nun who taught me in seventh grade at St. Alphonsus School in Greendale, Wisconsin. She was my first encounter with tyranny. She was a big believer in group punishment. When someone wrote on her blackboard "Sister Emerentia is a fascist," she announced the entire class would be detained after school until the culprit stepped forward. Even in seventh grade, I recognized that detention should be based on particularized suspicion. There were only two kids in that class who could spell "fascist," and they were the obvious suspects.

I had almost forgotten about Sister Emerentia until several years ago, when I discovered she had actually been appointed to the U.S. Supreme Court. There she was in the same black habit, announcing that all the seventh graders at Vernonia School in Oregon who wanted to play football would have to pee in a bottle. She signed the opinion Justice Antonin Scalia, but she didn't fool me.

Then a year later, I learned that Sister Emerentia had been elected governor of Georgia. She signed a law declaring that all candidates for public office in the State of Georgia must file a certificate declaring that they have been tested for illegal drugs and that the result of the test was negative. The Eleventh Circuit Court of Appeals upheld the law, concluding that "the nature of high public office in itself demands the highest levels of honesty, clear sightedness, and clear thinking." There's a lot of truth in that. It's hard to read a Gallup Poll when you are loaded. If we believe politicians can prove they are honest, clear-sighted, and clear thinking by peeing in a bottle, then we deserve all the pee we get. Fortunately, in this case, even Justice Scalia agreed the law was unconstitutional, and Georgia candidates for public office now need only certify that they have never had an extramarital affair.

For thirty years of hope and frustration, I have labored in the vineyards of academia, searching for a rational explanation for American drug policy. I began my academic career in 1970, the year that Richard Nixon announced we had turned the corner in the war on drugs. I have studied the science of chemistry and pharmacology, the psychology and etiology of addiction, the economics of wholesale and retail distribution, the ethics of the medical profession, and the jurisprudence of criminal punishment. I have reluctantly come to the conclusion that American drug policy does not really have much to do with science, psychology, economics, ethics, or jurisprudence. It has more to do with how politicians get elected. It has to do with media hype, plain and simple.

Our national debate on drug policy is dominated by twelve-second sound bites, devoid of thought but loaded with rhetorical zing. The suggestion that judges, legislators, and journalists approach this challenge by reading a book or studying a report or attending a conference and acquainting themselves with some credible factual information is greeted with horror. What, you want us to think about this problem? If the word got out that we were thinking, we would be labeled as "soft on crime."

It is a useless exercise to seek to engage the shapers of public policy in rational dialogue about drugs. When public opinion polls are so lopsided in identifying a demon and the demon has no credible defenders, no elected official in America has any interest in studying the demon when he or she can simply denounce it. The challenge now is to directly engage the public in rational dialogue and begin a process of withdrawal from their addiction to sound bites. In dealing with media-hype junkies, we must confront the denial that lies at the heart of their disease. That denial is, at its core, a denial of complexity. The fix that is offered by the purveyors of media hype is the seductive fix of simplicity. We must look for issues in which public policy has clearly been skewed by reliance on oversimplified media hype and let people see that they were deprived of some essential factual information before they made up their minds.

I am convinced there are at least two areas in which this is an achievable agenda: (1) mandatory minimum sentences and (2) sentence enhancements for recidivists. These are the two areas in which state

GERALD F. UELMEN

sentencing policies have been most adversely impacted by media drug hype.

Many states mandate minimum prison sentences for drug offenders based simply upon the quantity possessed or sold. These laws were based on the faulty assumption that drug dealers were an identifiable group that could be readily distinguished from drug users and that drug dealers could be deterred by the threat of draconian sentences. A national movement began during the 1970s with what was known as the Rockefeller Drug Laws in New York. Distribution of two ounces or possession of four ounces subjected the offender to a mandatory minimum prison sentence of fifteen years. That was supposed to scare drug dealers right off the sidewalks of New York.

A quarter century later, we start the new millennium with two million Americans behind bars, a disproportionate share of them young black men. More than one-third of these prisoners are drug offenders. We could treat most of them for one-third the cost of their imprisonment. In California, despite the investment of $5 billion in new prison construction, our prisons are bursting at the seams. More people are sent to prison for drug possession than any other crime. We now have 156,000 Californians incarcerated; and we spend almost as much on building, maintaining, and staffing our prisons as we do on our schools. The Correctional Peace Officers Association is the most powerful lobby in Sacramento, and they target for defeat any state legislator who advocates sentencing reform.

We truly have a "prison industrial complex" in California, and as a result, our public schools now rank among the worst in the nation. Twenty-five years ago, they were the best. In some states, the burdens of imprisonment costs are inspiring a reassessment of the wisdom of mandatory prison sentences for drug offenders. Since 1993, six states have repealed or reformed their laws. Among those advocating reform is the former state senator who cosponsored the Rockefeller Drug Law in 1973. John Dunne recently said, "It seemed like a good idea twenty-five years ago, but the sad fact is they haven't worked. They're ineffective, unfair, and extremely costly to taxpayers."

The other example is the more recent movement to enhance prison sentences for recidivists. The California "Three Strikes and You're Out" law is the harshest example, mandating life imprisonment for three-time offenders and tripling the sentence for second offenders. While ostensibly aimed at violent offenders, the law has most dramatically affected the sentences of those who served a previous sentence for a violent offense, then got rearrested (sometimes twenty-five years later) for a property crime or a drug offense. After five years of vigorous enforcement of this law, we now learn that we have added 4,121 lifers to our prison population, but 19 percent of them were simple drug offenders, and 32 percent committed only property crimes. The proportions are even higher for two-strike offenders, who end up serving three times as much time as they otherwise would; 31 percent of them are drug offenders.

How do we accomplish sentencing reform when politicians are immobilized by the pathological fear of a "soft on crime" label? In states that have the popular initiative, there is a way to go directly to the public with our arguments. And the public, we are discovering, can be persuaded.

Arizona led the way in 1996. Voters by a two-to-one margin passed the Drug Medicalization, Prevention, and Control Act. In addition to permitting medical use of marijuana, the law diverted nonviolent drug offenders into drug treatment and education programs rather than incarceration. The Arizona Supreme Court recently reported that the law is "resulting in safer communities and more substance abusing probationers in recovery," has already saved taxpayers over $2.5 million, and is helping more than 75 percent of program participants to remain drug-free.

In California, we have been inspired by the Arizona success. We approved a medical marijuana initiative in 1996, but it did not include the broader sentencing reforms of the Arizona measure. During the past three years, I have been deeply involved in the legal fight to implement the availability of medical marijuana despite the efforts of federal authorities to enjoin it. We will be back in front of the voters next November with another initiative measure, which will mandate that all nonviolent drug offenders be sentenced to treatment programs and will require that the proceeds of drug forfeiture laws be used to finance drug treatment programs. Currently, drug forfeiture proceeds just finance more police hardware to arrest more drug offenders. It will be poetic justice indeed to plow that money into drug treatment programs.

Another reason for optimism in California is the incredible success story of our drug courts. By setting up special courts to maintain continuing supervision over drug offenders, we are making progress

GERALD F. UELMEN

in breaking the cycle of shuffling addicts in and out of our jails. So after thirty years of frustration, I'm starting the new millennium with cautious optimism. The public can be educated, and the public can be persuaded to reform our drug sentencing laws. This is one issue where the people are ahead of the politicians. As for Sister Emerentia, she has announced that she is now a candidate to be president of the United States. Her campaign slogan is "Congress should be kept after school, and Bill Clinton should be spanked."

---

* From "The Impact of Drugs on Sentencing Policy," *St. Louis University Law Journal,* vol. 44, p. 359 (2000).

2

*U.S. v. Oakland Cannabis Buyers' Cooperative**

ARGUING A CASE before the U.S. Supreme Court is viewed by many as a pinnacle in a lawyer's career. I vividly remember the reverential awe I felt as a law student in 1964, watching cases argued at the high court and hoping that someday I would get a turn. It finally came in 2000, when Chief Justice William Rehnquist called the case of *U.S. v. Oakland Cannabis Buyers' Cooperative.*

As a law professor, I was able to combine the preparation of this case with an intense educational experience for twelve law students at Santa Clara University. The students helped research and write the brief. When the big day came, my students flew back to Washington and had front-row seats to watch the action.

As I sat down to reread the cases we were relying upon, I came across several I first read as a beginning law student. Among them was *The Queen v. Dudley*, a nineteenth-century British case used to illustrate the "necessity" defense in criminal law casebooks. It involved three sailors stranded in a lifeboat who survived by killing and eating a companion. The "necessity" defense was what our case was all about, but my current worry was that the justices would make a meal of me.

The court was reviewing a decision of the Ninth Circuit Court of Appeals, which ruled that an injunction closing down the Oakland club could be modified to allow distribution to a small group of patients who could demonstrate that they had serious medical conditions that could only be relieved by cannabis. Thus, there was no reasonable alternative available to them except to violate the Controlled Substances Act.

After granting a hearing, the Supreme Court granted the government's request for a stay of the modification to the injunction by a vote of 7–1, so we knew going in we were facing an uphill battle.

The government argued that the Controlled Substances Act allowed no exceptions whatsoever. Since Cannabis was placed on schedule I of the act, Congress had concluded there was no recognized medical use, and it could not be prescribed. Our response was that "necessity" should allow use without a prescription for patients who have no other alternative to avoid dire health consequences, including death.

I thought our strongest argument was that the government itself had permitted exceptions by setting up a Compassionate Investigative New Drug (IND) program to supply cannabis to seriously ill patients on an individual basis. In the early 1980s, they were supplying seventy-nine patients with cannabis cigarettes on a daily basis. Testimony before Congress clearly demonstrated that this was in fact a "medical necessity" program. In 1992, however, the program was shut down. No new applications have been accepted since then, although the government still continues to supply eight patients who still survive. The decision to close the program was a cynical response to a flood of new applications from AIDS patients.

In our brief, we traced the history of the Compassionate IND program and asked, "If the government can respond to medical necessity by providing cannabis to seriously ill persons, why should the Controlled Substances Act be construed to prevent us from doing the same thing?"

Four of the patients still being served by the government program signed a "friend of the court" brief.

In its reply, the government responded in arrogant fashion. In effect, it said, "We can do it because we're the federal government. You can't because you're a private party."

I decided that if I did nothing else in my oral argument, I wanted to respond to that display of government arrogance. An oral argument before the Supreme Court, however, lets the justices set the agenda. One must respond to the questions raised by the justices, and you are strictly limited to a half hour.

Justice David Souter leaned forward and addressed the first question to acting solicitor general Barbara Underwood. "Do you think we should take the case on the assumption that there really are some people for whom this is a medical necessity, or should we assume there are no such people?" Underwood calmly replied, "On the assumption that there are no such people." I felt annoyed and angry. The government was arrogantly asserting that the patients whose agony was described in sworn statements that were quoted in our brief did not even exist: we should just ignore them.

When my turn came, I was peppered with questions. When the white light flashed on, signaling that I had five minutes left, I felt a cold grip of panic. I had not yet said a word about the Compassionate IND program. A brief lull in the questions gave me the opportunity I needed. I raised my voice and launched into a passionate analysis of why the existence of the IND program was itself an admission by the government that medical necessity *can* provide an exception. The necessity defense requires that the defendant have no reasonable alternative but to break the law. As long as the government IND program existed, it provided a reasonable alternative. When the government shut off the safety valve, patients were left with no reasonable alternative, hence had a valid necessity defense. Thus, as private parties, we could now do what the government was refusing to do: respond to the medical needs of patients who faced life-threatening illness and had no other alternative for relief.

After the argument, one of the patients still enrolled in the IND program introduced himself. His name is Irvin Henry Rosenfeld, and he was diagnosed at the age of ten with a disease causing the continuous growth of bone tumors. He was treated with opioids, muscle relaxants, and anti-inflammatory medications, which helped little and produced debilitating side effects. He was admitted to the government program in 1982, and for nineteen years, the government had provided him with twelve marijuana cigarettes each day. He was a successful stockbroker handling multimillion dollar accounts. I thanked him for his courage in signing on to the brief so other patients could receive the benefit he had gained by getting access to the medicine he needed. It was a moving reminder of what the case was all about.

I left the courtroom with a sense of hope. After all the years of struggle against government intransigence, we were finally in a setting where rational argument and evidence could take one step further than media spins and political power plays. We were in the U.S. Supreme Court.

When the court's ruling and opinion came down on Monday, May 14, 2001, I was disappointed by the 8–0 loss but expected to see a reasoned rejection of our arguments. What I encountered instead was the same flaunting of federal authority. There was no acknowledgment that the government IND program ever existed. There was no attempt to explain why the Controlled Substances Act allowed it but would not allow Oakland to do the same. Those seventy-eight patients never existed.

The opinion was authored by Justice Clarence Thomas, who never made eye contact with me during the entire argument. He was looking at the ceiling the entire time. He didn't hear a word I said. It was not enough for Justice Thomas to say no to the Oakland Cannabis Buyers' Cooperative. He wanted to say no to all persons who might assert that any violation of any federal law was a lesser evil than their own suffering.

In a concurring opinion, Justice John Paul Stevens rejected a medical necessity exception for distributors such as our clients but left the matter open for patients themselves. Distributors, he said, thrust the choice of evils upon themselves by "electing" to assist suffering patients.

Not that long ago, we were debating whether states should enact laws to compel citizens to act as Good Samaritans. Now we were saying the Good Samaritan cannot stand in the shoes of those whose sufferings he alleviates. In other words, necessity is no defense if one's action is motivated by compassion.

What is compassion but to feel the suffering of others and seek to alleviate it? The court's message seems to be "Let's stick our heads in the sand and pretend that the sick and suffering who surround us are not there."

---

*   From *San Jose Mercury News,* April 1, 2001, and *San Francisco Chronicle,* May 20, 2001.

3

When Supreme Court Justices Enlist in a War*

THROUGHOUT OUR CONSTITUTIONAL history, the greatest atrocities that have been countenanced by the U.S. Supreme Court have been conducted "in the name of war." The suspensions of the writ of habeas corpus and trials of civilians by military tribunals during the Civil War, the jailing of strikers, the Palmer Raids, the censorship of the radical press in the wake of World War I, the internment of American citizens of Japanese ancestry during World War II—all these extraordinary exercises of government power were upheld under the banner of the power to wage war.

In his excellent book *In the Name of War*, Professor Christopher May finds some common threads running through all these cases. First is the total reliance by the court on information provided by the government to establish the necessity for its action. Frequently, such information is exposed as false many years later. But broad recognition of executive privilege precludes even *in camera* scrutiny of the basis for a claimed emergency.

Second, the courts are reluctant to challenge the leadership of the executive branch in a time of perceived national crisis. The president is in a stronger position to control the organs that generate the hysterical support of the public.

Finally, the court, like everyone else, simply likes to win wars. As Justice Robert Jackson put it, the Constitution in wartime "is interpreted by judges under the influence of the same passions and pressures" that affect their countrymen.

The current "war on drugs" is not an officially declared war against another country, so the constitutional power to wage war offers no justification for governmental action. Nonetheless, the U.S. Supreme

Court is displaying all the symptoms which Professor May finds characterize its war power cases. The justices repeatedly accept without skepticism the suggestions offered by the government that a national crisis of the greatest conceivable magnitude now besets us. The public hysteria whipped up by presidential politics has created a climate in which executive power akin to the power of a czar is broadly accepted, and even the deployment of troops is countenanced. And in the front ranks of this war, we find the enlistees include the justices of the Supreme Court, dismantling the protections of our Constitution to win victory over the scourge of drug abuse.

References to the urgency of national efforts to eradicate drug trafficking abound in Supreme Court opinions of the past decade. The usual sources offered to support these conclusions are law enforcement agencies, and the opinions inevitably cite each other in an unbroken string of bootstrapping. It began in *United States v. Mendenhall*, when a 5–4 majority upheld a warrantless strip search of an airline passenger by Drug Enforcement Agency (DEA) agents using a "drug courier" profile. The concurring opinion of Justice Powell, joined by Justice Blackmun and Chief Justice Burger, concluded that the detention of the defendant, a black female, by two DEA agents was justified because she arrived in Detroit from Los Angeles, was the last to get off the plane, walked slowly, and changed her reservation for a connecting flight. In emphasizing the public interest served by such seizures, Justice Powell stated,

> Few problems affecting the health and welfare of our population, particularly our young, cause greater concern than the escalating use of controlled substances. Much of the drug traffic is highly organized and conducted by sophisticated criminal syndicates. The profits are enormous.

Further references labeled drug trafficking a "serious societal threat." The authority cited for these conclusions were claims of the DEA quoted in a 1977 district court opinion. At the time Justice Powell wrote those words, illicit drug use by young people was beginning to decline.

Three years later, when the Supreme Court declared that the exposure of luggage to canine sniffing is not a search, the majority opinion of Justice O'Connor suggested that the government seizure of luggage on less than probable cause was justified by the "compelling interest in detecting those who would traffic in deadly drugs for personal profit." The authority the court offered to support its description of the menace of drug trafficking was Justice Powell's opinion in *Mendenhall*.

Two years later, the court handed down two major decisions accelerating further restriction of Fourth Amendment rights. In *New Jersey v. T.L.O.*, a holding that a junior high assistant vice principal could search a student's purse for marijuana without probable cause was justified by what was described as a compelling necessity to keep drugs out of school in order to control violence:

> Maintaining order in the classroom has never been easy, but in recent years, school disorder has often taken particularly ugly forms: drug use and violent crime in the schools have become major social problems.

The source cited by Justice White for the linkage of marijuana and violence in schools was a 1978 report of the U.S. Department of Health, Education, and Welfare titled "Violent Schools—Safe Schools: The Safe School Study Report to the Congress." The 247-page report never even suggests any linkage between drug use and school violence. To the contrary, although the report found school violence a serious problem in only 8 percent of the nation's schools (mostly in larger communities), it reported the availability of drugs substantially affects schools in all areas.

The same year, in *United States v. Montoya de Hernandez*, the court held that only a "reasonable suspicion" was required for incommunicado detention of a traveler from Columbia for sixteen hours, culminating in a rectal examination to search for cocaine. The majority opinion by Justice Rehnquist stressed the urgency of federal control of drug smuggling:

> These cases reflect longstanding concern for the protection of the integrity of the border. This concern is, if anything, heightened by the veritable national crisis in law enforcement caused by the smuggling of illicit narcotics.

Once again, the authority cited was Justice Powell's concurrence in *Mendenhall*. The bootstrapping culminated in the 1989 decision in *National Treasury Employees Union v. Von Raab*. In upholding a government plan requiring mandatory drug testing to analyze urine specimens taken from employees of the Customs Service, the court cited *Montoya de Hernandez* to elevate control of the drug problem to a place as "one of the most serious problems confronting our society today." As Justice Kennedy put it:

> The Customs Service is our nation's first line of defense against one of the greatest problems affecting the health and welfare of our population. We have adverted before to the "veritable national crisis in law enforcement caused by the smuggling of illicit narcotics."

In a pungent dissent, Justice Antonin Scalia pointed out that the government had failed to offer a single instance of drug use contributing to malfeasance by a customs officer. He suggested the real justification for the drug testing program was *not* to respond to any problems in the U.S. Customs Service, but to enlist its employees as "role models" for other government agencies and the private sector:

> What better way to show that the government is serious about its "war on drugs" than to subject its employees on the front line of that war to this invasion of their privacy and affront to their dignity? To be sure, there is only a slight chance that it will prevent some serious public harm resulting from Service employee drug use, but it will show to the world that the Service is "clean," and—most important of all—will demonstrate the determination of the government to eliminate this scourge of our society!

Rejecting the proposition that the end justifies the means, Justice Scalia concluded that the drug testing program was "a kind of immolation of privacy and human dignity in symbolic opposition to drug use."

Unfortunately, this lucid moment turned out to be only a brief interval for Justice Scalia. During the following term, in literally dismantling a half century of First Amendment jurisprudence in order to uphold the firing of Oregon employees who participated in a Native American religious ceremony including the use of peyote, Justice Scalia cited Justice Kennedy's opinion in *Von Raab* to declare the following:

Drug abuse is "one of the greatest problems affecting the health and welfare of our population," and thus "one of the most serious problems confronting our society today."

In dissenting, Justice Blackmun seemed to echo Justice Scalia's *Von Raab* dissent, suggesting that the ruling may be "a product of overreaction to the serious problems the country's drug crisis has generated," and stated that the state's interest "in fighting the critical war on drugs" was not the state interest to be weighed.

The common thread running through all these cases is the almost hysterical urgency to support and sustain government efforts to interdict the traffic in illicit drugs. All drugs are treated as though they pose the same threat: heroin, cocaine, marijuana, and peyote. And rarely, if ever, does the court even allude to the substantial literature that questions the hysteria being generated by federal law enforcement agencies.

Objective non–law enforcement reports and studies of the drug abuse problem have simply been ignored by the court. Probably the most comprehensive and illuminating national study of drug abuse ever compiled was that completed by the National Commission on Marijuana and Drug Abuse, chaired by former Governor Shafer of Pennsylvania. The commission—which included two senators, two congressmen, and nine professionals appointed by the president—issued two outstanding reports: "Marijuana: A Signal of Misunderstanding" was issued in 1972, and "Drug Abuse: Problem in Perspective" followed a year later. I find it absolutely incredible that in the subsequent forty years, neither report has ever been cited or referred to in any opinion of the U.S. Supreme Court.

Supreme Court opinions are replete with statements and assumptions about drug abuse that suggest the justices are simply not very well informed about the phenomenon of drug addiction and drug abuse. Obviously, their excuse is not that this information is classified or secret. Their ignorance seems a quite deliberate willingness to join the chorus, repeating the lines supplied by the law enforcement agencies that direct America's war on drugs. Perhaps the defense lawyers who appear before the court can be faulted as well for not making more of an effort to educate the justices in their briefs.

Forty years ago, I recall the eager anticipation I felt upon first learning of the discovery of endorphins. This monumental breakthrough in research of brain chemistry unlocked the key to understanding addiction and called the most basic premises underlying our criminal drug laws into question. Forty years later, you can run the word "endorphin" through LEXIS, and you will find the word does not appear in a single opinion of the U.S. Supreme Court nor even in an opinion of a federal circuit court of appeals. Obviously, the legal profession is sleeping through the current revolution in biochemistry. Unfortunately, so is the U.S. Supreme Court.

In October of 1986, journalist Adam Paul Weisman penned a classic confession in the *New Republic*. Titled "I Was a Drug Hype Junkie," it recounts his discovery that all the objective data proves that drugs became a *declining* national problem during the 1980s. The portrayal of drugs as the "nation's number one menace" by the national media emerges as a classic example of media manipulation to whip up public hysteria for political purposes. While it is sad to see *Time*, *Newsweek*, and U.S. News & World Report fall victim to this phenomenon, it is much sadder to see the drug hype appear in the opinions of the U.S. Supreme Court. As a result, our constitutional liberties have suffered grievously. They always do when the justices of the U.S. Supreme Court enlist in a war.

---

* From the *Champion*, National Association of Criminal Defense Lawyers, April 1991, p. 14.

4

Ruminations on Current Drug Policy

AS AN ADVOCATE for medicinal marijuana, I was well
aware that lots of recreational users were sneaking in under
the tent flaps. But I never saw the medical marijuana movement as
a stalking horse for complete legalization. I simply argued that the
existence of opioid abusers would never be offered as justification to
cut off availability of opioids to patients who needed to alleviate their
pain. Why should we treat those who find relief from their pain in
marijuana be penalized because others are using the drug for recreation?
The issue struck close to home for me because my own sister, who
was a quadriplegic confined to a wheelchair for her entire life, found
relief that she could not find elsewhere for the peripheral pain she
experienced by consuming marijuana. Despite her disability, my sister
Jean earned a PhD, assisted many others as a therapist, achieved her
ambition to become a mother, and lived out her life in Guatemala,
where she cofounded a library to bring literacy and computer skills to
the children of Dueñas.

Despite losing the Oakland Cannabis Club case, I had a part
to play in the ultimate vindication of medicinal marijuana through
my representation of WAMM, the Wo/Men's Alliance for Medical
Marijuana in Santa Cruz, California. WAMM is a legitimate medical
marijuana collective, serving patients who used the drug to alleviate
the side effects of cancer treatment or the wasting syndrome of AIDS.
For me, representing Valerie Corral, the founder of WAMM, was like
representing Mother Teresa. She is the most compassionate person I
ever met. After the DEA raided WAMM, we went to federal court to
seek an injunction to prevent the federal authorities from interfering

with its operations. The case was settled with an agreement by federal authorities to leave WAMM alone.

After the frustration of watching the federal war on drugs become a federal war on medical marijuana, it was a great relief to see a modicum of sanity return to our national drug policy with the election of Barack Obama and the appointment of Attorney General Eric Holder. The new federal policy of leaving it up to the states to regulate access to marijuana and calling off federal interference with those who are in full compliance with state law makes perfect sense. With respect to the legalization of recreational use undertaken by Colorado and Washington, however, I am somewhat skeptical. First, I see conflicts emerging regarding the continuing availability of medical marijuana. Can legitimate patients be exempted from the substantial taxes being imposed on marijuana production and distribution? Will the continued availability of medical marijuana be jeopardized by recreational users seeking to avoid the taxes by claiming medical need? Second, I concede the need to keep this drug out of the hands of youngsters but fear we will be no more successful in doing so than we have been with cigarettes and alcohol. Third, I worry that marijuana producers and sellers will demand the same First Amendment rights that allow tobacco manufacturers and alcohol producers to promote their products. By turning over the production and sale of recreational marijuana to private entrepreneurs, whose goal is to maximize their profits, we will replicate the continual menace that big alcohol and big tobacco represent. Their profits come from the 10 percent who are the heaviest users, and their marketing strategy is to turn users into heavy users.

I also applaud the Obama administration for the reform of drug sentencing laws it has promoted. The Fair Sentencing Act finally addressed the hypocrisy of a 100 to 1 ratio between crack cocaine and powder cocaine in handing out mandatory prison sentences. Hopefully, we are moving closer to treating drug addiction as a medical problem and offering treatment as an alternative to jail sentences.

VII

A Sense of Humor

1

The Mating of Apes

M Y CLAIM TO honor as the poet laureate of O. J. Simpson's "Dream Team" had some precedents. One of my first attempts at poetic humor was in response to an assignment in my freshman English class at Loyola University in 1959. Professor Ted Erlandson rewarded my effort with an A.

> He swings from a tree to caress her;
> To his whining, she finally grunts, "Yes, sir."
> If Darwin was right,
> From this clash in the night
> Will evolve a Loyola professor.

2

The Fifth Freedom

A NOTHER EFFORT CAME later that year as I embarked upon my study of political science. The issue of pay toilets had not yet achieved the public attention it gained fifteen years later, when Dr. March Fong Eu kicked off her successful campaign to be elected California secretary of state by smashing a toilet bowl on the steps of the California capitol, arguing that pay toilets discriminated against women since men's urinals were free or men could at least just go find a tree.

In speeches and essays and pamphlets galore,
Four Freedoms we boast of and multitudes more.
We speak and we pray without fear of arrest,
And press or assembly is seldom suppressed.
They're all guaranteed in the Bill of our Rights,
These ratified, glorified, fought for delights.
But lately I've noticed that something was missed,
When Adams and Jefferson wrote up that list.
They overlooked one thing we can't do without;
A function that Bills of Rights don't speak about.
Yet each of us daily must heed nature's call;
Retreat to that porcelain bowl on the wall.
When urgency beckons, all men should be free;
But this, greedy gas stations somehow can't see.
Their toilets are locked, on the door is a sign:
"Deposit Ten Cents." (But I only have nine).
In the land of the free, it indeed is a crime,
That poor weary travelers must borrow a dime.
If Congressmen will not consider our plight,
Just one course is left to regain our lost right.
We cannot go on with exorbitant fees:
Let's picket the pay toilets; head for the trees!

3

The Saga of Steve Miller

I AGAIN CLAIMED the mantle of poet laureate during the years I served as an assistant U.S. attorney in Los Angeles. The duties of this exalted position required the composition of memorial poems to mark the departure or retirement of fellow assistants in the office. I thought my best effort was made on behalf of Steve Miller, a very gifted attorney with whom I shared an office in the Division of Organized Crime prosecutions.

Three years had passed since he came West to the California sun.
In three years with the U.S. attorney, every trial was won.
But now he faced the toughest test in the war against organized crime;
The trial of Sam the Bookie, a man who had never done time.
A hush fell over the courtroom as Miller strode through the door;
The defendant cowered and quaked with fear when he rose to take the floor.
The gallery was packed with young ladies, whom Steve had invited to see,
The day of his greatest glory when Sam would no longer be free.
He winked at the court reporter, to the judge gave a wave of the hand;
To one and all, it was plain to see Steve Miller was in command.
Facing the jury, he pointed at the frightened bookie's face;
"An animal out of the jungle!" he screamed. "Convict this public disgrace!"
The jury was back in ten minutes with a verdict to be read:
"We recommend the defendant to be hanged by the neck until dead."
Steve's record remained unblemished; justice, as always, was done:
When asked by the press for a comment, he said only, "Gee, it was fun!"

Then he drove off into the sunset, in the direction of Beverly Hills;
Hollywood starlets would flock to his door, with money for contracts
and wills.

But one day he will return again, and Assistant U.S. Attorneys will
tense,

As he stands at the calendar call to announce, "Stephen Miller . . .
for the defense."

Evidence (To the Tune of "Camelot")

DURING MY YEARS of teaching as a law professor at Loyola Law School in Los Angeles, the students presented a Libel and Slander Night, when they presented skits making fun of their professors. The faculty usually retaliated with their own skit, and I frequently contributed a song or two. For example, the year that Mary Poppins scored a hit, I put on a general's uniform and sang "A Law Professor Must Be a General" to mimic the patter song "A British Nanny Must Be a General." But my best effort was singing the glories of the course in evidence for a skit presenting a faculty curriculum committee meeting in which professors were competing for which of their courses should be awarded the most units. It was sung to the tune of "Camelot," which was then still a big hit on the Broadway stage. In my subsequent years of teaching evidence, both at Loyola and Santa Clara, I always ended the course by asking students to join me for a sing-along of this song:

A law was passed a distant moon ago here,
A code which doesn't make a lot of sense;
But every student of the law must know it
It's Evidence.

When opposing counsel puts on his star witness,
And judge and jury listen too intense,
It's time for lots of frivolous objections
From Evidence.

Evidence, Evidence
Sometimes it may seem like a lot,

But in Evidence, Evidence,
You'll learn objections on the spot.

The character of a witness may be challenged,
By conviction of a felony offense,
But not if it's a minor misdemeanor
In Evidence.

The hearsay rule has numerous exceptions,
Including one for dying declarants;
But only if the truth is what's asserted
In Evidence.

Evidence, Evidence
You can recite the federal rules;
And in Evidence, Evidence,
Make your opponents look like fools.

When there's danger that the truth may be exposed,
You must object on grounds of relevance;
A limiting instruction should be given
In Evidence.

And when you're in the courtrooms of our nation,
In the daily war for dollars and for cents,
You'll use the tricks we taught, by clients you'll be sought;
And always you'll be grateful for our course in Evidence!

GERALD F. UELMEN

5

Confessions of a Former Freeway Fibber

WHEN I MADE the move from teaching at Loyola Law School in Los Angeles to become dean at Santa Clara University School of Law four hundred miles to the north, I was thrilled about the reduction this would mean for my freeway commutes to and from work each day. With tongue in cheek, I put my gloating into an op-ed column, which was published in the *Los Angeles Times* on December 14, 1986:

> For 16 years I drove the Harbor Freeway from San Pedro to the Ninth Street exit downtown. Every day. Both ways. And for 16 years I lied. "You live in San Pedro? That must be an awful commute." "Oh, it's not that bad. Usually half an hour. Of course, I don't have to travel during the peak rush hour." In the entire 16 years I made it in half an hour once. That was when I had to go in at 4 o'clock on a Sunday morning. Once, captivated by talk about the "window" between peak rush hours, I tried going in at 2 p.m. and coming home at 10 p.m., only to discover that my informants lied a lot, too.
>
> I don't know why I never owned up to the truth. It's not as if I was trying to entice people to move to San Pedro. I didn't even realize how much lying I was doing until my redemption came in the form of a move 400 miles north to Santa Clara, where part of the inducement was a distance to work so short that it could hardly be called commuting.
>
> When I realized the extent of my prevarication, I undertook a scientific survey of other L.A. commuters. I discovered that all L.A. commuters lie about the length of their commute, and that the extent of their lies can be ascertained by a simple formula: Multiply time

they tell you they spend on the freeway by 125%, and add a minute and a half for each year they've been commuting.

Psychology offers cogent explanations for why 7 million people would all lie to each other. Denial, we are told, is a natural part of the grieving process. By denying that a loss has occurred, we give our psyche time to build up enough resources to cope with reality. That's how we cope with losses such as baldness, forgetfulness, an expanding waistline and wrinkled skin. Since those are losses that keep accumulating, we have to keep denying. Our line of denial is always 10 yards behind reality.

Somehow, an expanding girth or a receding hairline is easier to accept than an increase in commuting time. I have grown ready to acknowledge that I am losing *some* hair, and that I've put on a *few* pounds. But I could never bring myself to admit that each year another minute-and-a-half was added to my commuting time. When I started in 1970, I lied that it took 30 minutes when it really took 37. When I finished in 1986, I was telling the same lie, "usually 30 minutes," when it really took 61.

I've occasionally met Angelenos who use the length of their commute to rationalize all sorts of extravagances. They need a more luxurious automobile than they can really afford because they "spend so much time in the car." That's why they also need a telephone in the car, and a $2,000 stereo system. When they're backed into a corner, though, and confronted with the ultimate question—how long does it take you?—they still lie.

The realization that lying about your commuting time is part of the L.A. life style may explain why rapid transit will never become a reality in L.A. If commuters began traveling by train, their lies could be exposed by the simple expedient of checking the train schedule.

I am not making this public confession to purge the guilt of a troubled conscience. I'm satisfied that my 16 years of lying was harmless enough. Nobody believed me anyway. Nor am I seeking to suppress a coping mechanism that may be essential to survival in L.A. All I hope to accomplish is to reestablish my own credibility. Now that I have left L.A., I've joined the ranks of supercilious expatriates who come back to visit and boast about how little time they now spend commuting. What sheer joy to see the jealous looks on the faces of my old L.A. friends when I tell them about my new

GERALD F. UELMEN

commute. Invariably, though, their jealousy turns to suspicion. I see them mentally computing to compensate for the L.A. fudge factor. They immediately assume that my new commute is double what I claim.

Am I stuck forever with the L.A. commuter credibility rap?
I *swear*, door-to-door now, it's only 10 minutes.
Of course, I don't have to travel during the peak rush hour.

6

Alas, David Souter
Won't Read This

O UT OF ALL the op-ed columns I authored (including over twenty that were published in the *Los Angeles Times*), I only made the *New York Times* once. That was in 1980, when David Souter was up for confirmation for a seat on the U.S. Supreme Court. When I read that he was not a frequent reader of newspapers, I couldn't resist another tongue-in-cheek contribution.

The media portrayal of Judge David Souter as a recluse from the back woods of New Hampshire raises a serious question about his fitness for the Supreme Court.

Previous Republican nominees brought to the court an acute sensitivity to the problems of the common people, acquired through years of membership in exclusive country clubs. They were exposed to the hurly-burly of American political life by serving as volunteer poll watchers to challenge the voting credentials of minorities. But Souter doesn't seem to socialize much at all, and apparently even avoids town meetings.

Most shocking of all, Souter does not watch television, listen to the radio or read any newspapers save the Sunday edition of the New York Times. While this might speak well for his intelligence, what does it say about his ability to function at Washington cocktail parties?

Having a justice on the highest court who doesn't read the daily newspapers presents grave potential for acute embarrassment. In fact, one of the most embarrassing moments in the life of the great Justice Oliver Wendell Holmes was directly attributable to his lack of attention to the morning papers.

Before his appointment to the high court, Holmes presided over a state court in Massachusetts, where he was called upon to rule on a motion for a continuance of a murder trial filed by a lawyer named Swasey. Twirling his mustache, Holmes began to pontificate:

"Mr. Swasey, the record shows that the trial of this case has at your request been continued once. Last summer, when I was in England visiting the law courts, Mr. Justice Stephen commented to me on the importance of speedy trials in the administration of justice, particularly in capital cases while witnesses were available, evidence fresh in the mind, and before suggestions could create false psychological memories."

As Holmes paused before ruling, Swasey inquired, "Has your honor read the morning papers?" An annoyed Holmes inquired what bearing the morning papers could possibly have on the motion. "None," replied Swasey, "but they do report that yesterday Mr. Justice Stephen was judicially committed to an institution for the feeble-minded." Amidst harrumphs, Holmes granted the motion.

Souter will find little comfort in offering Holmes as his role model, however. Holmes was a bon vivant, and one of his letters to Sir Frederick Pollock suggests he did read what the newspapers had to say about his own nomination to the U.S. Supreme Court: "The New York Evening Post, I see, says that I have not been a great judge, being brilliant rather than sound." In fact, it was Holmes who also said, "The life of the law has not been logic; it has been experience."

Regular reading of newspapers is essential for a justice to be in touch with the pulse of the public. As Oscar Wilde put it, "By giving us the opinions of the uneducated, modern journalism keeps us in touch with the ignorance of the community."

We must also bear in mind that as a justice of the Supreme Court, Souter will be a guardian of the First Amendment, which protects freedom of the press.

Souter obviously needs to be reminded that the wisdom of our founding fathers gave newspapers an important place in American life. As Thomas Jefferson said, "Were it left to me to decide whether we should have a government without newspapers, or newspapers without a government, I should not hesitate a moment to prefer the latter."

But he said that in 1787, before he ran for president. After he was president, and read what the newspapers had to say about him, Jefferson said, "The man who reads nothing at all is better educated than the man who reads nothing but newspapers."

In a speech this summer, Justice Antonin Scalia excoriated news reporters for their shallow coverage of court decisions. He concluded with the judgment: "No news is good news." If Judge David Souter is confirmed, there will be at least two votes on the Supreme Court for that late Jeffersonian viewpoint.

7

Ruminations on Legal Humor

F ROM THE TIME I started law school, I have been collecting
    books of legal humor. Of the eight books I have authored or
coauthored, the most successful have been two collections of legal
humor. During the past twenty-five years, there has been a virtual
explosion of websites and blogs devoted to legal humor. One might
conclude from all this that people like to laugh at lawyers, but I believe
a better explanation is that lawyers love to laugh at themselves.

I leave you with my two favorite jokes. First is one I frequently tell
after the person introducing me to give a speech informs the audience
that I play the accordion. I reply that I love being asked to play my
accordion; and for many years, I carried it around in the backseat of
my car, hoping someone would ask me to play. But several months
ago, when I returned to the parking lot, I found the window of my car
was broken . . . and there were two accordions in the backseat. I love
to watch the faces in the audience as their initial feelings of sympathy
for my loss turn to roars of laughter. Then I tell them that they need
not worry that I might start playing the accordion. After all, I am a
gentleman. A gentleman is someone who can play the accordion but
doesn't.

My other favorite was also the favorite of Justice Stanley Mosk,
who always started a speech with a joke. He related the story of the
prosecutor at the arraignment of a defendant who said to the judge,
"This man was married to three women at the same time. We are
charging him with bigotry." The judge responds, "That's not bigotry,
you idiot. That's trigonometry!"

VIII

My Heroes

1

Clarence Darrow*

MAY A LAWYER resort to bribery and espionage when confronted with an adversary who regularly and brazenly engages in bribery and espionage to defeat him or her? Apparently, Clarence Darrow thought so. When placed on trial for bribing a juror in the *McNamara* trial in Los Angeles in 1912, Darrow challenged the jury hearing his case to acquit him even if they believed he did arrange for jurors to be bribed:

> Suppose you thought that I was guilty, suppose you thought so—
> . . . would you dare to say by your verdict that scoundrels like [the district attorney] should be saved from their own sins, by charging those sins to someone else? . . . Now, gentlemen, I am going to be honest with you in this matter. The McNamara case was a hard fight.
> . . . Here was the District Attorney with his sleuths. Here was Burns with his hounds. Here was the Erectors' Association with its gold. A man could not stir out of his home or out of his office without being attacked by these men ready to commit all sorts of deeds. Besides, they had the Grand Jury, we didn't. They had the Police Force, we didn't. They had organized Government, we didn't. We had to work fast and hard. We had to work the best we could, and I would like to compare notes with them.

Darrow returned to this theme in discussing the testimony of Guy Biddinger, a Burns detective who testified that Darrow passed $500 in cash to him in an elevator in exchange for information about the prosecution's investigation of the McNamaras:

> Of course, I did not pass $500 in the elevator, but if I had, I had just as much right to give that $500 for that purpose as I would have

to buy $500 worth of hogs, just exactly. I was doing exactly what they were doing, what Burns admitted he was doing, what was done in all their cases, what Sam Browne says they did, when he testified that they filled our office with detectives. And here comes this wonderful man, so honest, so pure, so high, so mighty, [District Attorney] Ford, who says the State has a right to do that, who says the State has a right to put spies in the camp of the "criminal," but the "criminal" hasn't the right to put spies in their camp. Isn't that wonderful, gentlemen? Here is a contest between two parties in litigation; the prosecution has a right to load us up with spies and detectives and informers, and we cannot put anyone in their office. Now, what do you think of that? Do any of you believe it?

Darrow's rhetorical question is still a zinger ninety years later. The jury acquitted him in the face of overwhelming evidence of guilt, strongly suggesting that they agreed with his argument that his underhanded techniques were no worse than the underhanded techniques of his opponents. Ninety years later, what do we think of a legal system that permits the prosecution to bribe witnesses, backdoor judges, and kidnap defendants and engages in spying and eavesdropping on defense lawyers but severely punishes defense lawyers who engage in the same conduct? When is it appropriate to fight fire with fire?

Clarence Darrow served as lead counsel in at least four cases that have been labeled "trials of the century," but the two cases that placed him in the center of ethical storms both involved charges of deadly terrorist activity by labor union leaders. In the summer of 1907, Darrow successfully defended William D. Haywood, leader of the Western Federation of Miners, on a charge of murdering the former governor of Idaho, Frank Steunenberg, who was killed by a bomb planted at the front gate of his home. In the winter of 1911, Darrow went to Los Angeles to defend brothers James and John McNamara, labor organizers who were charged with planting a dynamite bomb in the printing plant of the *Los Angeles Times*, a strident anti-union newspaper. The explosion on October 10, 1910, killed twenty *Times* employees. The trial ended when the defendants entered pleas of guilty shortly after Darrow's chief jury investigator was arrested while passing a bribe to a juror.

In a letter to U.S. Attorney General George Wickersham, the attorney in charge of a federal probe of the *LA Times* bombing conspiracy summed up the misconduct that the investigation of Darrow's defense on behalf of the McNamaras had turned up: two jurors bribed; two witnesses paid to get out of the country; two witnesses paid to testify falsely; a corrupt scheme to destroy certain physical evidence in the possession of state authorities; the corruption of practically every employee of the Los Angeles County Jail who came in contact with the McNamaras; complicity in a scheme of to get the wife of one of those indicted for the *Times* murder, and still being secreted, out of the state; the hiring of an uncle of Ortie McManigal to induce the latter to repudiate his confession on the personal guarantee of Darrow that McManigal would be made a free man; and other minor irregularities almost too numerous to mention.

Evidence of most of these activities was offered in the course of Darrow's trials for bribing jurors. Darrow denied most of the activity, but the denials wore thin as the evidence accumulated. Darrow's defense placed increasing reliance on a theory of justification: he was fighting fire with fire.

With the exception of the bribery of jurors, every offense in this litany could be matched with equally offensive conduct by the prosecution. From Darrow's perspective, the prosecution even enjoyed the advantage of a rigged jury: The judge was a member of the most elite club in the city, and anyone who did not own property and was not acceptable to the prosecution would not be allowed on the jury. The jurors all knew that they would be rewarded for voting to convict the McNamaras and punished if they voted for acquittal. In voting to set Darrow free, juror Golding once noted, he acted "contrary to my best interests (from a mercenary standpoint)." The forces of capital bribed jurors too, but the approach was a bit more subtle. Perhaps Darrow's perspective was the problem. He saw the world as his clients saw it: a massive struggle by labor to cast off the chains of oppression imposed by the forces of capital. In an 1895 address he titled "The Right of Revolution," Darrow had said,

> The high motive of the revolutionists is one side, the strength of the government to protect itself is the other. . . . Victor Hugo, in his immortal work, Les Miserables, sends the kind priest to reason with the old dying revolutionist, who sat on the porch of his hermit's cottage, waiting for night and death, which were coming side by side. The priest upbraids him for the cruelty of the revolution; the

old man rouses from his dying stupor and says: "You speak of the revolution-a storm had been gathering for fifteen hundred years; it burst, you blame the thunderbolt." . . . With the land and possessions of America rapidly passing into the hands of a favored few; with great corporations taking the place of individual effort; with the small shops going down before the great factories and department stores; with thousands of men and women in idleness and want; with wages constantly tending to a lower level; with the number of women and children rapidly increasing in factory and store; with the sight of thousands of children forced into involuntary slavery at the tender age that should find them at home or in the school; with courts sending men to jail without trial for daring to refuse to work; with bribery and corruption openly charged, constantly reiterated by the press, and universally believed; and above all and more than all, with the knowledge that the servants of the people, elected to correct abuses, are bought and sold in legislative halls at the bidding of corporations and individuals: with all these notorious evils sapping the foundations of popular government and destroying personal liberty, some rude awakening must come. And if it shall come in the lightning and tornado of civil war, the same as forty years ago, when you then look abroad over the ruin and desolation, remember the long years in which the storm was rising, and do not blame the thunderbolt.

Darrow's respectable liberal friends were not surprised when he was charged with bribing jurors. They realized that Darrow believed the end could justify the means. One even wrote to him, "If by any chance you did [take a long chance for your clients], I am certain that you did nothing that any other lawyer would not have done placed in the same position in such an important case." Others were not so forgiving. The poet Edgar Lee Masters, himself an idealistic young lawyer who assisted Darrow in the McNamara case, penned a devastating portrait of the moral character of Darrow in 1916:

You can crawl / Hungry and subtle over Eden's wall, / And shame half grown up truth, or make a lie/Full grown as good. . . . A giant as we hoped, in truth a dwarf; / A barrel of slop that shines on Lethe's wharf, / Which seemed at first a vessel with sweet wine /For thirsty lips. So down the swift decline / You went through sloven spirit, craven heart / And cynic indolence. And here the art / Of molding clay has caught you for the nonce / And made your head our shame-your head in bronze! One thing is sure, you will not long be dust / When this bronze will be broken as a bust / And given to the junkman to re-sell. / You know this and the thought of it is hell!

The most that can be said in Darrow's defense is to ask the question he himself asked the jurors who tried him: should scoundrels like the prosecutors "be saved from their own sins by charging those sins to someone else?" The detectives and lawyers who prosecuted the Haywoods and McNamaras of a century ago were also zealots. They clearly believed that the culprits they pursued were mortal enemies of society, the terrorists of their time. And they were ready to pull out all the stops to eliminate them by fair means or foul. In this respect, little has changed in one hundred years.

The justification of "fighting fire with fire" may seem more appropriate to the battleground than to the courtroom, but in both settings, the participants are expected to play by the rules. Even in war, the use of weapons like poison gas cannot be justified by the fact that one's opponent used poison gas first. Both sides would be guilty of a war crime, although it is ordinarily the one who loses the war who is held accountable for his war crimes.

One of the ironies of Clarence Darrow's early career is that the shady dealings in which he engaged in Los Angeles were probably no different from the way he conducted himself in prior cases. Even before the Los Angeles events, there was widespread suspicion that jurors in the Haywood trial had been bribed. Darrow played to win, knowing that the risks of being held accountable for breaking the rules were much higher for losers. Darrow's reputation for pushing the ethical envelope certainly had a lot to do with the heightened scrutiny that police and prosecutors applied to his defense team in the McNamara trial.

This immediately identifies a serious problem with "fighting fire with fire." Over an extended period of time, everyone forgets who set the first fire. The Los Angeles prosecutors probably justified their use of spies and informants in the defense camp because they were sure Darrow would deploy spies and informants against them. From this perspective, they were the ones who were fighting fire with fire. Thus, fighting fire with fire invites a constantly escalating conflagration with diminishing ability to sift through the ashes and determine who started it.

The phenomenon of "loser pays" can also provide us with some insights. An ongoing trial resembles a war in many important respects, but one crucial similarity is the need to suspend any serious investigation of rule breaking until the shooting has stopped. While charges and countercharges of unethical behavior are frequently exchanged in the midst of high-profile trials, an immediate investigation of these charges would seriously impede the ongoing trial process. The temptation is greatest to engage in conduct that crosses ethical lines when that conduct is perceived as sealing a victory. Then a winner can deflect a subsequent investigation as sour grapes or retribution on the part of a sore loser. This phenomenon is frequently observed during election contests, where charges and countercharges of unethical campaign conduct cannot be resolved prior to the election and often disappear when the election is over.

Going beyond our battlefield and electioneering analogies, the role of a courtroom advocate carries the unique obligation of unswerving loyalty to the client. This duty requires a lawyer to withdraw when he or she has conflicting loyalties to other clients or to one's own self-interest. One of the gravest risks of fighting fire with fire is the potential for the lawyer himself to become an accused, with a need to defend himself, which may conflict with his duty of loyalty to his client. Darrow faced this problem when his chief jury investigator was arrested at the outset of the McNamara trial. It is generally believed that the quick and surprising change of plea by the McNamaras was engineered to provide Darrow with a defense to the charges of jury bribing. What need would there be to bribe jurors if the McNamaras were going to plead guilty? Darrow contended that the decision to change the plea preceded the arrest of his investigator. If the change of plea was motivated by Darrow's need for a defense, the McNamaras were denied the effective assistance of counsel. Their lawyer had an irreconcilable conflict of interest between his own interests and theirs.

The unfair advantages that the prosecution enjoyed in Darrow's trials were already the object of scrutiny and criticism in Darrow's time. Private funding of the prosecution was concealed from public view precisely because it was widely perceived as unfair and unethical. The use of private detectives was the object of frequent criticism and was beginning to receive legislative attention. The most effective way to bring about reform would have been to expose these practices whenever possible. One seriously undercuts his ability to function as a "reformer," however, when he engages in the very same practices himself. Thus, another drawback of fighting fire with fire is that the prospects for meaningful reform are diminished.

Except that it might enhance your chances of winning, fighting fire with fire has little to recommend it. But for some, winning is everything, and the end justifies the means. Sadly, it appears Clarence Darrow in 1911 was one of those for whom winning was everything. He did not seek victory just to gratify his own ego, however. He strongly identified with his clients and the cause of labor. Is fighting fire with fire justifiable when the success of a higher cause is at stake? What if the cause is perceived as the greatest cause imaginable—the cause of survival of one's highest values? That question must be answered by returning to the limited role cast for advocates in our adversary system. An advocate who is a zealot for a "higher cause" is rarely competent to function as a lawyer. He or she simply lacks the independent perspective that is essential to exercise good judgment on behalf of a client. The lawyer who fights fire with fire to serve a higher cause is not serving that cause well and lacks the perspective to even recognize the harm he is doing to his client. Ultimately, the cause itself will be ill served by fighting fire with fire. Short of a successful revolution, a cause that is advanced by corruption simply will not gain the public support essential to success in a democracy.

This reflection on the ethics of Clarence Darrow has led me to an unanticipated conclusion. My personal hero—the man who inspired my own ambition to become a lawyer—turns out to have been not just unethical, but a lousy lawyer to boot. By fighting fire with fire, he ended up not only burning himself, but he seriously damaged the cause of labor as well. If Clarence Darrow's career had ended in 1911, he would surely be consigned to the hell of ignominy portrayed by the poetry of Edgar Lee Masters. But Darrow lived for another twenty-six years, and during that period, he pursued a very different direction in his legal career. He never represented the cause of labor again, but the causes he took up were just as important. He truly redeemed himself and gained his place as an inspirational role model for future generations of lawyers.

Even Edgar Lee Masters recognized this and authored another later poem about Clarence Darrow:

> There were tears for human suffering, or for a glance / Into the vast futility of life, / Which he had seen from the first, being old / When he was born . . . / This is Darrow, / Inadequately scrawled, with his young, old heart, / And his drawl, and his infinite paradox, / And his sadness, and kindness, / And his artist sense that drives him to shape his life / To something harmonious, even against the schemes of God.

When we emulate the ideals of Clarence Darrow, it should not be by fighting fire with fire. It should be by directing a steady stream of water on the fires that still smolder today, replicating the injustices of a century ago. The "well-meaning men of zeal" who are ready to burn up our constitutional liberties in order to enhance our security are with us today, just as they were a hundred years ago. The way to defeat them is by the kind of advocacy that Darrow demonstrated in the courtrooms of Dayton, Tennessee, and Chicago, Illinois: advocacy that turned the hearts and minds of an entire generation—not by fighting fire with fire, but by fighting ignorance and hate with wisdom and love.

---

* From "Fighting Fire with Fire: A Reflection on the Ethics of Clarence Darrow," *Fordham Law Review,* vol. 71, p. 1543 (2002–2003).

2

William Jennings Bryan*

I SAW THE film *Inherit the Wind* for the first time sixty years ago before I became a lawyer, and I loved it. In some respects, becoming a lawyer ruined the film for me. Not much that goes on in the film resembles a real trial, and some of the theatrics now seem hokey. Also, in the course of writing a one-man play about the life of William Jennings Bryan, I spent considerable time reading accounts and transcripts from the actual trial the film is supposed to depict. That ruined the film even more, realizing how many liberties were taken with actual events.

The film is loosely based on the events surrounding the 1925 trial of John Scopes in Dayton, Tennessee, for teaching Darwin's theory of evolution to high school students. Rather than ruin the film for you by pointing out all the legal and historical inaccuracies, I decided to write an essay on why this film is still great entertainment, just like the Scopes trial itself was great entertainment. There's truly something refreshing about unabashedly treating a trial as a circus. To some extent, every trial is a potential circus, but we rarely set out to make it one. In Dayton, Tennessee, in 1925, they did. And they succeeded to an extent unparalleled in American history.

Today, labeling a trial as a "circus" is rarely intended as a compliment. Trials are supposed to be taken quite seriously by everyone involved, and the lawyers are supposed to focus their persuasive powers on the judge and the jury, not the peanut gallery. At several key moments during the trial as portrayed in *Inherit the Wind*, the lawyer characters based on Clarence Darrow and William Jennings Bryan actually turn their backs on the judge and jury and address remarks directly to the appreciative courtroom audience, which cheers, hisses, and provides a cacophony of catcalls. Real lawyers would never do that. But at some point, I'm sure, Stanley Kramer said, "What the hell, these aren't real lawyers, anyway."

With respect to Bryan, he was probably right. I discovered several points in the transcript of the Scopes trial where Bryan forgot he was arguing to a judge and punctuated his oratory with frequent references to the listeners as "my friends."

Ironically, the current movement to ban television cameras from courtrooms in the wake of the O. J. Simpson trial is based on the premise that the cameras are like the Sirens of old—seducing the lawyers, witnesses, and even the judge to play to the television audience, thus turning the trial into a "circus." Television cameras can have that effect. Witnesses may testify as if they're performing a gig. Lawyers may trade cheap shots to provide sound bites for the evening news. The judge may delay his most dramatic rulings until prime time.

Some of the most amusing moments in *Inherit the Wind* depict media coverage of a trial in the age before television. The judge is frequently interrupted by explosions of flash powder. The newspaper reporters, including Gene Kelly portraying a character based on H. L. Mencken (with more dapperness and charm than Mencken ever mustered), loudly dictate their stories into telephones right from the courtroom as the proceedings unfold. They receive glowering glances from the lawyers whose performances they pan. And a huge microphone is brought into the courtroom to broadcast the verdict over the radio, setting off a shoving match among the trial participants to hog the microphone. It reminded me of one wag's comment that the most dangerous place in a courtroom is to stand between Alan Dershowitz and a television camera. As depicted in *Inherit the Wind*, the most dangerous place in the courtroom is between Matt Brady (a.k.a. William Jennings Bryan), played brilliantly by Fredric March, and the WGN microphone. When the microphone is removed, Bryan drops dead on the spot. H. L. Mencken attributes his death to a "busted belly," but the symptoms more closely resemble a severe reaction to adulatory deprivation, also known as F. Lee Bailey disease.

The Scopes trial was deliberately designed to be a three-ring circus, so no one was critical or disappointed when it became an entertainment extravaganza. Actually, the arrest and trial of John Scopes was cooked up by the town fathers in Robinson's Drugstore, one block from the Dayton courthouse. I got a chance to visit Dayton thirty years ago and was thrilled to discover the courtroom preserved just as it appears in 1925 photographs. Visiting the town was like walking through a time warp. Robinson's Drugstore was still there, and it was still called Robinson's Drugstore. We met Mr. Robinson, who was the eight-year-old son of the drugstore proprietor when the Scopes trial took place.

Inherit the Wind does a masterful job of exposing the underlying motives of civic boasting that pervade the trial. Henry Drummond (a.k.a. Clarence Darrow), portrayed by an overweight Spencer Tracy, is recruited by a newspaper to serve as defense counsel precisely because his presence will produce newsworthy fireworks. Volunteer prosecutor Matt Brady is welcomed to town with a big parade, complete with brass band playing "Old Time Religion." The town fathers are thrilled that the little hamlet of Hillsboro will host an event every bit as exciting as "the Chautauqua in Chattanooga."

Without some drama and some romance, however, a circus movie can get boring. *Inherit the Wind* serves up generous portions of drama and romance, and that's where the film parts company with the historical events that actually occurred in Dayton. While the trial tested the validity of a state law prohibiting the teaching of "evil-looshen," as all the hayseed characters portrayed in the film pronounce it, not much was really at stake for John Scopes. He faced a small fine if convicted, and William Jennings Bryan offered to pay the fine for him if the ACLU didn't. John Scopes was a great admirer of Bryan, who was the commencement speaker at his high school graduation. The movie seeks to build a little more suspense by portraying a dramatic arrest of Bert Cates, the character based on Scopes, and keeping him in jail throughout the trial. And Matt Brady is portrayed bitterly protesting when Cates is not sent to prison after his conviction.

The most dramatic incident in the film never happened in the actual trial. Matt Brady calls Bert Cates's fiancée to the stand and forces her to reveal Bert's irreverent musings about religion to the jury. Brady almost salivates as he presses the reluctant young lady to "tell it, tell it, tell it!" There's not much subtlety here. The good guys are the "thinkers." Spencer Tracy ends the film by professing his secret belief in God, his secret admiration for Matt Brady, and his secret contempt for E. K. Hornbeck, the Mencken character. Then he slams the Bible and Darwin's *On the Origin of Species* together and strides out of the courtroom. The bad guys are all loony yokels and bigots, portrayed in much the same way the media now portrays the Buchanan wing of the Republican Party.

The high point, just as it was the high point of the Scopes trial, comes when Henry Drummond calls Matt Brady to the witness stand and cross-examines him on his literal interpretation of the Bible. While some of the questions used were actually put to Bryan by Darrow, the movie depicts Brady as a bumbling bigot who crumbles under Drummond's onslaught.

It's fun to watch, but nothing like what really happened. Bryan actually angered some of his supporters from the Bible Belt by conceding that the seven days in which the creation of the world is described in Genesis may not have been twenty-four-hour days but may have been periods of thousands of years, thus accepting the possibility of a reconciliation of evolutionary theory and divine creation. Bryan also delivered a zinger to Darrow by pointing out that while Darrow labeled Tennessee parents "yokels" for seeking to control the teaching of Darwin in public schools, Darrow himself just one year before put the blame for Loeb and Leopold's murder of Bobby Franks on the University of Chicago because the university taught Loeb and Leopold the philosophy of Nietzsche. Within a single year, the "great defender" attacked the University of Chicago for corrupting his murderous clients by teaching from the books of one philosopher, then attacked the State of Tennessee for seeking to prevent the "corruption" of its youth by teaching from the books of another philosopher. Perhaps Darrow would explain that it depends on the current popularity of the philosopher in question. Or perhaps he would insist that consistency is a hobgoblin. In any event, the circus portrayed in *Inherit the Wind* casts Darrow as the ringmaster and Bryan as the clown. Bryan's reputation was ruined by both the movie and the play on which it was based. The film is every bit as entertaining as a trip to the circus and should be relished in that spirit. But history it ain't. The "trial of the century" known as *People v. John T. Scopes* featured plenty of circus clowns, but William Jennings Bryan was not among them.

My fascination with Bryan began in high school, where I encountered the "Cross of Gold" speech for the first time. Sixty years after he gave it, the speech was still a staple of high school "oratorical interpretation" competitions in which I participated. When I became serious about focusing my eclectic collecting interests, I picked up as many Bryan buttons as I could afford. I was especially impressed by the fact you could actually watch a candidate age, from the handsome strapping thirty-six-year-old who bowled over the Chicago convention of the Democratic Party in 1896 to the bald, overweight warhorse who won his third nomination at the Denver convention in 1908. I began to include Bryan biographies in my collection and read them all. Bryan himself turned out a half-dozen books and edited his own newspaper, the *Commoner*. I discovered he was a gifted writer and began to sense why he acquired such a devoted following of admirers.

In 1987, after I became the dean of Santa Clara University School of Law, I arranged to bring an actor-lawyer to our campus to present the one-man play about Clarence Darrow, made famous by Henry Fonda. The actor was Donald Fiedler of Omaha. When I picked him up at the airport, I was blown away. He was the spitting image of William Jennings Bryan! Wearing a wig, he made a convincing Darrow; but I gave him a button from my collection so he could see his uncanny resemblance to Darrow's nemesis, Bryan. At that moment, the seed was planted in my brain. The appropriate vehicle to resurrect William Jennings Bryan would be a one-man play!

I had long been a devotee of the one-man play, especially admiring James Whitmore's portrayal of Harry Truman in *Give 'Em Hell, Harry*. (Truman's boyhood hero, incidentally, was William Jennings Bryan.) When I retired from the deanship in 1994, I resolved to devote my yearlong sabbatical to finally writing a one-man play on the life of William Jennings Bryan. My sabbatical plans were slightly disrupted by the invitation to join the defense team being assembled for the Los Angeles trial of O. J. Simpson. I soon found, however, that I needed an occasional escape from my own involvement in a "trial of the century." Bryan became my escape, a project in which I could be totally immersed and occasionally turn off the media obsession with the Simpson trial. The writing of the play became a true "labor of love." Playwrights, I discovered, have greater license to put words into people's mouths than lawyers; but I was initially reluctant to have Bryan speak words that he had never spoken in his lifetime. As I gained confidence that I could embellish Bryan's words without betraying the truth of who he really was, the play took off. As it got closer to an actual production, the opportunity to do readings and assess audience reaction greatly enriched the script. We actually staged a reading of the play in a Sunset Strip theater in the midst of the Simpson trial, with the entire "Dream Team" in the audience. Ed Asner performed the reading, and I saw

Bryan come to life again for the first time. My goal was to have the play performed in Chicago during the 1996 Democratic Convention, the one hundredth anniversary of the "Cross of Gold" speech. The speech provides the climax of the first act of the play.

As soon as the script was complete, I sent it to Donald Fiedler in Omaha. He took it to Charles Jones, the artistic director of the Omaha Community Playhouse, and they became enthusiastic boosters for an Omaha premiere. In June of 1996, the play opened for a two-week run in Omaha, with Don playing Bryan. Charles Jones and his wife, Eleanor, designed the set and codirected the production. The reviews were encouraging, and the audiences were very appreciative. An even bigger thrill came for me when the play was taken to Lincoln, Nebraska, Bryan's hometown. We had an opening night reception in Bryan's family home, Fairview, which has been beautifully restored on the grounds of Bryan Health.

In August, we moved the Omaha production to Chicago's Touchstone Theatre to have it run during the Democratic Convention. Those who attended the Chicago performance received a souvenir button, replicating one of my favorite Bryan buttons, the 1908 "From Lincoln to Washington" slogan. While the play received enthusiastic reviews, we found our sparse audiences were mainly drawn from Chicago's traditional theater crowd. Although we scheduled daily matinees, we discovered few convention goers could be lured away from the nonstop partying to celebrate Clinton's renomination to attend a play, even if the play depicted some great moments in American political history and even if the play offered much better oratory than the insipid speeches wafting from the podium at the United Center.

An especially poignant moment came for me when an elderly lady called the Touchstone Theatre and invited me to her apartment. She had a remarkable story. Her mother was an artist, and some of her paintings were hung in the Bryan home. When I visited her, she presented me with a pristine studio portrait of Bryan as a young congressman, which Bryan himself had presented to her mother.

We ended the year with a one-week run at our campus theater at Santa Clara for appreciative hometown audiences. But Bryan's territory will always be America's heartland, where William Jennings Bryan is still remembered the way the poet Vachel Lindsey portrayed him:

I brag and chant of Bryan, Bryan, Bryan, Bryan.
Candidate for president who sketched a silver Zion.
The one American poet who could sing outdoors,
He brought in tides of wonder, of unprecedented splendor,
Wild roses from the plains, that made hearts tender,
All the funny circus silks, Of politics unfurled,
Bartlett pears of romance that were honey at the cores,
And torchlights down the street, to the end of the world.

---

* From "The Trial as a Circus," *University of San Francisco Law Review,* vol. 30, p. 1222 (Summer 1996) and "Bringing Bryan to Life," *Political Collector,* vol. 26, no. 10 (June 1997).

3

Justice Stanley Mosk*

THE LIFE OF Stanley Mosk has much to teach us about politics and justice in America. It also offers a window into historic struggles that still reverberate in our times. Decades of scholarly attention given to Los Angeles and California history have barely noticed the evidence demonstrating that Stanley Mosk stood at the center, or very close to it, of the epochal, defining moments during seven decades of the last century. The longest-serving justice in the history of the California Supreme Court (1964–2001), he possessed a unique combination of political savvy, personal charm, sharp intelligence, and talent as a judge. But even before he became a justice of California's high court, Stanley Mosk was a force to be reckoned with. From his arrival in California in 1933, he was fully engaged in the civic, social, and political life of his community, state, and nation.

As a neophyte lawyer during the Depression years, he allied with radical and progressive civic leaders, investigating and publicizing police brutality and labor violence. He helped to catalyze a grassroots movement for municipal reform in Los Angeles during the 1930s, playing an instrumental role in the nation's first successful recall drive to oust a corrupt big city mayor, Frank Shaw. His efforts on behalf of farmworkers and labor unions as well as the alliances he forged led to Mosk being labeled a "communist sympathizer," and for two decades, he successfully defended himself against the label that sidelined many aspiring political leaders.

His first political appointment began what came to be a sixty-four-year career in public service. Democratic governor Culbert Olson appointed Mosk as executive secretary, where he often took center stage as the voice of the governor's office and, among other duties, briefed Olson about clemency appeals from death row inmates. On the eve of his departure from office, Olson appointed Mosk to the Los Angeles

Superior Court, the youngest person ever named to that bench. His sixteen-year tenure on the superior court captured a broad swath of public attention. As a family court judge, he made headlines presiding over scores of cases involving Hollywood celebrities like Judy Garland, Lana Turner, and Charlie Chaplin. The press followed his every move, and when he briefly left the bench to enlist in the U.S. Army as buck private, they dubbed him GI Judge. Returning to his seat, Mosk spoke widely about problems facing veterans and new African American residents to the region, such as access to housing and jobs. In 1947, he issued a precedent-shattering ruling declaring racially restrictive covenants unenforceable under the U.S. Constitution. His indefatigable community activism, a weekly newspaper column called "Judging the News," and his leadership posts in local affiliates of secular and Jewish national organizations made him a popular figure and a Jewish icon. This allowed him to help forge a political alliance among white liberals and African Americans that transformed Los Angeles and California politics.

Skillfully building upon this base, Mosk was elected as attorney general of California in 1958. He won with the largest margin of victory of any contested candidate in the nation that year, which was a remarkable achievement for a superior court judge. As the first Jew elected to statewide office since the gold rush era, Mosk demonstrated that being Jewish could be a political asset in California rather than a liability. Despite the climate of lingering McCarthyism, he warned citizens against the threat to freedom and civil liberties from extremist right-wing groups, the threat to the constitutionally protected separation of church and state from religious zealots, and the threat to the rights of labor and consumers from powerful corporate conglomerates.

At each stage of his political and judicial career, Mosk dealt with recurring issues facing Californians and Americans in general in a volatile climate of anticommunist hysteria, racial conflict, government corruption, and rampant abuse by law enforcement officials. While earning the wrath of FBI director J. Edgar Hoover, Los Angeles Police chief William Parker, and like-minded minions of law and order, Mosk remained sensitive to the need to balance the crime-fighting goals and methods of law enforcement against the liberty of individual citizens. He worked closely with U.S. attorney general Robert Kennedy to help formulate national policy regarding illicit drugs and promoted a new framework for the nation's attorneys generals to rein in the abuse of power by law enforcement agencies.

In the midst of the unprecedented dynamic growth of California, Mosk seized every opportunity available to advance the causes of justice and tolerance. As a citizen activist, judge, political office holder, and supreme court justice, he dedicated his life to protecting civil liberties and civil rights through advocacy, public policy, and the promotion and interpretation of state and federal law. Nearly every political campaign of note, from the rise of Earl Warren and Richard Nixon, through the administrations of Governors Goodwin Knight, Pat Brown, Ronald Reagan, Jerry Brown, George Deukmejian, Pete Wilson, and Gray Davis directly involved Stanley Mosk in one way or another. California chief justice Phil Gibson was a mentor throughout Mosk's career, from his days as a law student through his tenure on the supreme court. Governor Pat Brown and Assembly Speaker Jesse Unruh were political enemies, but both were friends of Stanley Mosk. President John F. Kennedy and Attorney General Robert F. Kennedy were close allies, and Mosk's emulation of their playboy lifestyle cost him dearly. His intimate friendship with William Clark, President Reagan's secretary of the interior, was an odd coupling of a staunch conservative and an unrepentant liberal. Presidents, governors, and senators valued his counsel; and local and state officials called upon his intellect and experience. He touched the lives of thousands—some famous, some obscure, some infamous—as he journeyed throughout the tumultuous years of the last century.

His life was not without controversy. Mosk's political popularity nearly propelled him to a seat in the U.S. Senate, an ambition that was quashed by an embarrassing lapse in his private life. In 1964, at the height of his political career, with polls suggesting a slam dunk victory and the late president Kennedy's endorsement, Mosk readied his followers to help him win the Democratic nomination for the U.S. Senate. Some even speculated he would soon have a shot at a vice presidential slot. Many still believe Mosk's withdrawal from the Senate campaign changed the course of California history and paved the way for the political ascendency of Ronald Reagan.

Stanley Mosk's political ambition, however, was vulnerable to a half decade of spying and intelligence gathering by the FBI and the

LAPD. Motivated by J. Edgar Hoover's obsession with the "communist menace" and Los Angeles Police chief William Parker's zeal to identify threats to his visions of law and order, both agencies engaged in extensive surveillance of many public officials, especially those who were most outspoken in promoting respect for our constitutional values. While many of the day-to-day observations or accounts of Mosk's activities reflect events that parallel newspaper and other published accounts, the accuracy of descriptions by others and the interpretations drawn by undercover agents should be read skeptically within the context of the unbridled abuse of government resources, power, and reach administered by Director Hoover. Similarly, details derived from a 1960s report on detainees in custody of the Los Angeles Police Department do not purport to reflect truth, but they do reflect the LAPD's perceptions of events that helped to change the course of history. Justice Mosk's devotion to the right of privacy and the need for courts to enforce constitutional limits upon investigative activities by police may well have found inspiration in his own victimization.

Speculation abounded about the timing of Governor Pat Brown's appointment of Stanley Mosk to the California Supreme Court. It now appears clear that a seat on the supreme court was Mosk's consolation prize for agreeing to withdraw from the Senate race. Regardless of how he got there, Mosk's intellect, personal charm, and keen political sensibilities enabled him to survive several retention elections. With encouragement from long-standing supporters, he occasionally toyed with returning to partisan electoral office, even as he carved out a historic legacy on the court. As a justice of the most respected state supreme court in the nation, Stanley Mosk achieved national prominence for his reasoned arguments and brilliant prose, and his formulation of the Mosk Doctrine became a leading force in the revival of a modern interpretation of "states' rights." This doctrine of state constitutionalism advocates state constitutions rather than the federal constitution as the primary ground for state supreme court decisions, insulating state court decisions from review by an increasingly conservative U.S. Supreme Court.

A stalwart opponent of racial quotas, Mosk challenged the policy of affirmative action, suffering through an abusive backlash from his liberal "friends." As a reviewing judge, he bowed to the overwhelming public will to uphold the death penalty while carefully evaluating its fairness and accuracy. Many of his judicial opinions are still regarded as "landmarks," forging changes in the law that have stood the test of time. Throughout his tenure, he was often a dissenting voice, criticizing the course taken by the court majority.

As the longest-serving justice in the history of the California Supreme Court, Stanley Mosk possessed a rare combination of political acumen and talent as a judge. The court faced formidable opposition from powerful special interests that could finance expensive initiative campaigns. In 1986, under the auspices of opposition to the court's rulings in death penalty cases, their efforts led to the bitterest judicial election contest in the nation, which culminated in a purge that swept Chief Justice Rose Bird and Associate Justices Cruz Reynoso and Joseph Grodin off the bench. Justice Stanley Mosk survived that election and managed to stay in office through many more years of political turmoil. Although his career path was singular, it can teach us a great deal about the politician as a judge in our legal system as well as the need for every judge to be a "politician" of sorts.

Justice Mosk was not aloof from controversies—winning some and losing some, but always emerging with his reputation for thoughtfulness and fairness intact. There were times, of course, when he felt discouraged. "The Goddess of Justice is wearing a black arm-band today, as she weeps for the Constitution of California,"[1] he wrote in one memorable dissent. Despite disappointments, he continued to exhort his fellow judges and fellow citizens to "recognize what can be changed and what cannot."[2] Mosk's passion was tempered by political pragmatism, and his acceptance of practical limits distinguishes his judicial philosophy from other "liberal" judges.

Personally, Stanley Mosk has been described as shy, smart, charming, ambitious, witty, optimistic, and resourceful. He has also been described as cunning, duplicitous, opportunistic, elitist, and sexist. Some aspects of his life remain enigmatic. Viewing his life in its entirety, however, he emerges as a principled idealist, who truly valued liberty, equality, and justice and who, at every stage of his expanding influence, used the power of his position to ensure these values for the larger good.

Ultimately, Justice Stanley Mosk was "one of that breed, few in number" that were not only skilled craftsmen, but also "architects" of the law. "Judges who are capable of perceiving how the particular case

GERALD F. UELMEN

and the particular issue fits into the overall structure of the law; or, more broadly, . . . how it fits within the framework of institutions and values that define our political community."

Stanley Mosk's life is a window into the larger demographic, social, and political changes in California that helped to shape the cases coming before the court. Mosk arrived on the high court in the midst of a social revolution, when America's traditions, leaders, and authorities were often under attack. His tenure lasted until the new millennium, which found Californians still dealing with many of the same issues as it struggled with new challenges posed by advancing technology, political polarization, and the declining quality of the environment.

The California Supreme Court has long been recognized as the nation's leading state supreme court due in large measure to strong leadership by its judicial giants. Justice Mosk knew them all and now stands tall among them. To many, his death in 2001 signaled the loss of one of the last of the great liberals in a conservative era. In an era when nearly every court in the nation struggles to balance sharply different judicial philosophies, the life and career of Justice Stanley Mosk offers us a unique perspective into the dynamic interplay of law, politics, and justice in America.

---

* From *Justice Stanley Mosk: A Life at the Center of California Politics and Justice,* Gerald Uelmen and Jacqueline Braitman, McFarland (2013).

4

Chief Justice Rose Bird*

ALMOST THIRTY YEARS after she left the court and fifteen years after her death, the legacy of Rose Bird is still shrouded with controversy. I considered myself a friend of Rose Bird and was a very active campaigner for her in the 1986 retention election that ended her judicial career. While researching and coauthoring the biography of Justice Stanley Mosk, I gained some insights into what was really going on behind the scenes of her turbulent chief justiceship.

Rose Bird grew up in poverty in New York, with her mother barely scraping by after being abandoned with three children by Rose's father. Her mother's courage was a great example for her. Rose was very bright and a diligent and ambitious student. She earned her bachelor's degree magna cum laude from Long Island University. After graduation near the top of her law school class at the University of California at Berkeley in 1965, Rose Bird spent a year clerking on the Nevada Supreme Court. Then she joined the Santa Clara County Public Defender's Office, where she tried cases, argued appeals in both state and federal court, and taught part-time at Stanford Law School. It's interesting that the Nevada Supreme Court was reputed to be one of the most dysfunctional state supreme courts in the country, and that was Rose's only exposure to the inside workings of the judicial branch. Rose never married, sharing a home in Palo Alto with her mother. When Jerry Brown announced for governor, she volunteered to assist his campaign and frequently chauffeured him to and from campaign events in the Bay Area. Brown was impressed by her outspoken independence. Brown won a narrow victory and immediately invited Bird to serve on his transition team, then named her to his cabinet. She spent two years at the helm of the California Department of Agriculture, the first woman appointed to a cabinet-level position in California. Her tenure was marked by both courage and controversy. Under her leadership, the state banned use of the short-handled hoe, which had inflicted disabling injuries upon generations of migrant farmworkers. Her work in drafting the landmark Agricultural Labor Relations Act finally gave the state's farmworkers a meaningful right to organize unions to bargain for higher wages and better working and living conditions. During her service in the governor's cabinet, she was diagnosed with breast cancer and underwent a modified radical mastectomy in 1976. The cancer returned after her retirement from the court, and after enduring another mastectomy in 1996 and several operations after, she declined further life-maintaining treatments and died in 1999 at the age of sixty-three.

In early 1977, Governor Jerry Brown was presented with three vacancies on the California Supreme Court in rapid succession, giving him a unique opportunity to put his stamp on the court for years to come. Incredibly, that opportunity has come twice in his lifetime.

Brown was eager to make the first appointment of a woman to the state supreme court and place her at the head of the court, sending a clear message that he was "shaking up" California government from top to bottom, rejecting the "old boy" politics of his father. But the first woman Brown looked to for this appointment was not Rose Bird. It was Shirley Hufstedler, who after a stellar career as a judge on the U.S. Court of Appeals for the Ninth Circuit was then serving as President Jimmy Carter's secretary of education. Shirley turned the appointment as chief justice of California down for the obvious reason that she was then considered the leading candidate for Jimmy Carter's first appointment to the U.S. Supreme Court. It's one of the real ironies of history that Jimmy Carter never got to make an appointment to the U.S. Supreme Court. If he had, the first woman on the court would not have been Sandra Day O'Connor. It would have been Shirley Hufstedler.

Brown's announcement that his choice would be Rose Bird was greeted by great controversy because of her lack of judicial experience. For a time, it looked as though the three-person Commission on Judicial Qualifications would not approve her appointment. The commission was chaired by Justice Mathew Tobriner as acting chief justice, who was a strong Bird supporter. The longest-serving court of appeals justice also served on the commission. At that time, it was Parker Wood, who regarded judicial experience as an essential qualification for any appellate appointment and for that reason voted against Bird. The determinative vote would be cast by Attorney General Evelle Younger, who was then gearing up to run against Governor Brown in the next election. Nineteen of the twenty-three Republicans in the State Assembly and seven of the fourteen Republican senators signed letters urging Younger to vote against Bird. Roman Catholic bishop Roger Mahony, then of Fresno, who served Governor Brown as first chair of the Agricultural Labor Relations Board, addressed a confidential letter to Justice Tobriner, expressing grave misgivings about her appointment, based upon personal experience. He wrote, "She has a personal temperament which enables her to lash out at people who do not agree with her. Her normal approach is to become vindictive, then to transfer her feelings to a long phase of non-communication. She would refuse to take or return telephone calls or to acknowledge any attempts at communication." Ultimately, Attorney General Younger "reluctantly" voted to confirm Rose Bird, issuing a backhanded statement that "the law does not require [the governor] appoint a judge or the best-qualified or even a well-qualified person. My limited responsibility requires only that I determine if Rose Bird is qualified. Absent any significant evidence to the contrary, I am compelled to find that she is."

Probably the person who was most disappointed by Rose Bird's appointment was Associate Justice Stanley Mosk, who clearly thought the appointment should have gone to him. Justice Mosk did not attend the festive swearing in of Rose Bird by Governor Jerry Brown. He never spoke to Governor Brown again. After she arrived at the court's headquarters in San Francisco, Mosk said to her, "I certainly cannot blame you for being here, but I blame Jerry Brown for putting you here." The relationship between Chief Justice Rose Bird and Justice Stanley Mosk was frosty and formal from the start and never got much warmer. Years later, when Rose Bird made an offhand comment about seeing how late Justice Mosk was working from the light in the transom over his office door, Justice Mosk called in carpenters to board up the transom. While Justice Mosk certainly deserves his stature as one of the greatest justices to serve on the California Supreme Court, his appalling treatment of Rose Bird is a wart that should not be covered up.

Chief Justice Rose Bird displayed aggressive confidence in her administrative skills, with little inclination to seek advice from or initiate consultation with her fellow justices. At the court, she installed former students from Stanford Law School as executive assistant and law clerk. Unlike her predecessor, Don Wright, whose door was always open to fellow justices and their staffs, Chief Justice Bird was available only by appointment prearranged with her executive assistant, who always sat in on her meetings, taking notes. This created resentment and isolated her from the friendly banter in the hallways.

The California Supreme Court was confronted with some hot-button issues in the short interval between Bird's 1977 appointment and her initial confirmation election scheduled for November 1978. At the primary election on June 6, 1978, the voters adopted Proposition 13, a popular measure that gave most homeowners an immediate one-third reduction in their property taxes. The measure was challenged on constitutional grounds, and the court granted an immediate hearing. On September 22, 1978, the court issued a 6–1 decision upholding the constitutionality of the measure. Chief Justice Bird authored a solo dissent, arguing that the widely differing tax assessment of property of equal value, depending upon when it was acquired, violated equal protection of the laws. Chief Justice Bird's dissent was very courageous, knowing how popular Proposition 13 was. Her vote to strike it down hardly enhanced her popularity with the voters.

The other hot-button issue was a challenge to a popular "use a gun, go to prison" law enacted by the legislature in 1975. At the time, judges had full discretion in robbery convictions to sentence defendants to state prison or to place them on probation. The "use a gun, go to prison" law was intended to eliminate that discretion and *require* a sentence to state prison in any case where it was alleged and proven that a gun was used in the commission of the offense. In *People v. Tanner*, a defendant who was convicted of robbery with the use of a gun argued that the law requiring a sentence to prison did not override another section of the penal code that gives a judge discretion to *dismiss* a criminal charge. The power to dismiss the charge, it was argued, included the power to dismiss a part of the charge. Thus, the sentencing judge would have discretion to dismiss or strike the allegation that a gun was used in the commission of the offense and sentence the defendant to probation. This argument was accepted by the superior court, then reversed by the court of appeals.

Tanner then filed a petition for a hearing in the California Supreme Court, which was granted on July 21, 1977. The court did not hear oral argument in *Tanner* until November 2, 1977, still one full year before the confirmation election. On March 3, 1978, Justice Tobriner sent his colleagues a proposed majority opinion. That opinion was not announced until eight months later, *after* Rose Bird had been narrowly confirmed in the closest retention election in the court's history. On the morning of election day, an article appeared in the *Los Angeles Times* claiming release of the decision had been deliberately delayed until after the election by Justice Mathew Tobriner, identified as "one of Ms. Bird's strong supporters against a well-organized campaign to win voter disapproval of her appointment to the court."

Two weeks later, Chief Justice Rose Bird released a letter she sent to the chairman of the Commission on Judicial Performance, requesting the commission to undertake an investigation into whether the *Tanner* decision had been improperly delayed and to issue a public report of detailed factual findings and conclusions. Significantly, she assured him, "As soon as the decision in the *Tanner* case is announced and has become final, you will be provided all necessary access to the internal records of the Supreme Court relevant to your inquiry." She took this action on her own initiative without discussing the advisability of this course with the court or seeking their concurrence in her waiver of the secrecy of the court's internal operations. Justice Mosk filed a successful suit to suspend the public hearings of the commission and then testified in a closed hearing.

When all the evidence was in, it was clear that there was no evidence to support a finding of impropriety by any justice of the court; and the commission so reported in a cryptic conclusory report, complaining that the decision in *Mosk v. Superior Court* not only prohibited it from concluding the hearings in public but also prohibited public dissemination of the analysis and reasoning employed in arriving at a disposition of the proceedings. The exoneration sought by Chief Justice Bird for Justice Tobriner eluded her, and court's public image was badly tarnished. A siege mentality prevailed at the court as political efforts continued to unseat the chief justice. A petition to force her recall was circulated in 1981 by a group of disgruntled prosecutors. Six more recall petitions were circulated in 1982. None of them qualified for the ballot, but the anti-Bird efforts made Rose Bird very wary of the media and suspicious of her "enemies" on the court.

For the California Supreme Court, 1986 was destined to be a political donnybrook. In an unusual combination of circumstances, the entire court, with the sole exception of Justice Allen Broussard, would appear on the November ballot for confirmation or retention. George Deukmejian was a candidate for a second term as governor in 1986 in a rematch with Los Angeles mayor Tom Bradley, the Democratic candidate he defeated in 1982. The governor's opposition to Rose Bird became a centerpiece of his gubernatorial campaign.

The issue that would define the campaign to remove Rose Bird would be her voting record on death penalty cases. Fifty-nine death penalty appeals had come before the California Supreme Court since the enactment of Deukmejian's bill to restore the California death penalty in 1977. And Chief Justice Rose Bird had voted to reverse every one of them! The governor also targeted Justices Cruz Reynoso and Joe Grodin based on their reluctance to affirm death penalty judgments. The governor's use of death penalty votes as a criterion in selecting his targets underlined an irony that is essential to an understanding of what happened to the court in 1986. The targeted justices were subjected to a well-funded campaign to remove them from office. The chief contributors to that campaign were corporations and insurance companies who believed Governor George Deukmejian would appoint replacements who were friendlier to their business interests. The entire campaign, however, was focused on the justices' voting record in death penalty cases. Television ads suggested that votes against the retention or confirmation of Chief Justice Bird, Justice Reynoso, and Justice Grodin would be "three votes for the death penalty." The strategy succeeded. In the November election, Governor Deukmejian roundly defeated Mayor Tom Bradley. Chief Justice Bird was rejected, winning approval of only 33.8 percent of the voters. Justices Cruz Reynoso and Joseph Grodin were also removed from office by a narrower vote.

Rose Bird's campaign for retention suffered from the same defects as her leadership of the court: obsessive control of every aspect of the campaign, combined with paranoid secrecy and mistrust of the media. While her supporters mounted a vigorous campaign to uphold judicial independence, they were outspent by more than $5 million. In the end, even a majority of California judges voted against Bird's retention. Justices Reynoso and Grodin found it impossible to separate themselves from the chief justice. While they mounted separately funded campaigns, the anti-Bird forces succeeded in linking their fate to that of the chief justice.

The replacement justices whom Governor Deukmejian then appointed to the California Supreme Court clearly got the message the voters had delivered. From 1979 through 1986, the Supreme Court of California reviewed sixty-four judgments of death. Five of them, or 7.8 percent, were affirmed. From 1987 through March of 1989, the Supreme Court of California reviewed seventy-one judgments of death. Fifty-one of them, or 71.8 percent, were affirmed. In two short years, the California affirmance rate for state supreme court review of death penalty judgments moved from the third lowest in the United States to the eighth highest. Subsequent appointments brought it even higher to 95 percent, the highest death penalty affirmance rate in the country. It's interesting to reflect on the impact those changes had on the population of California's death row. In 1985 and 1986, prosecutors were getting a clear message from the supreme court to ease up on the use of the death penalty, and the numbers started to decline. After the election, the numbers went back up through the ceiling, currently topping out at 751.

After her defeat, in her farewell remarks, Rose Bird said, "How am I taking this? My answer is, just like a man." She then added, "It is possible to have a house of justice, not a house of puppets. It's not a house of politicians, not a house of powerful interests, but in fact, a house of justice. And most importantly, not a house of death, but a house of justice."

Ten years after her humiliating ouster from the bench, Bird remained at the fringe of the legal community and, some say, of society. She was found working as a volunteer running the copy machine at the Stanford Law School poverty law clinic. She had become a reclusive figure, fearful at times for her safety and convinced that her public vilification made it impossible for her to represent clients. She was then not even licensed to practice law in California. After her death, the association California Women Lawyers established the Rose Bird Memorial Award, annually awarded to a woman for excellence as a jurist and for long-standing and/or groundbreaking public service and inspiration to women lawyers in California. Her personal courage was never in doubt, but her tenure demonstrated that a modicum of political skills is essential for success, even as a judge.

---

* From remarks delivered at Thomas Jefferson Law School Women and Law Conference, March 27, 2015.

GERALD F. UELMEN

5

Edward Bennett Williams

ONE OF MY personal heroes has always been Edward Bennett Williams, who defended Senator Joseph McCarthy, alleged racketeer Frank Costello, union leader Jimmy Hoffa, and many other famous "villains" of the era in which I grew up. My biggest thrill as a student at Georgetown Law School was to argue (and win) a moot court case in which Edward Bennett Williams sat as a judge. His dignity, wit, and eloquence provided a powerful role model. When I graduated from law school, I proudly presented my father with a copy of *One Man's Freedom*, a wonderful book written by Williams in 1962. In it, he documented that the history of civil liberties in America has been written in its criminal courtrooms and that whenever the government infringes on individual rights, it begins with "the weak and the friendless, the scorned and degraded, or the nonconformist and the unorthodox." Even with youthful stars in my eyes, I realized this litany was not always a perfect match with the list of clients Edward Bennett Williams represented. But nearly all his clients were scorned and publicly reviled as villains. And Edward Bennett Williams was frequently scorned and reviled along with his clients.

Here is how I inscribed the book to my father:

Dad—

This book expresses, as well as anything I've encountered, the ideals to the advancement of which I hope to dedicate my career as a lawyer. I feel its an appropriate gift for you, Dad, because you, more than anyone else, have instilled these ideals in me by inspiring their basic foundation: faith in the ultimate goodness of mankind, and compassion for his failings. That's the richest legacy any father can leave his sons. Thank you for it.

Your loving son,

Jerry

My dad's response stunned me. He wrote to say he was glad to hear I had come to a decision about my future career, commenting he was confident I would be a lot happier in criminal law "than the staid work of corporation law." *But* he underlined:

> I don't care very much for your hero Edward Bennett Williams. No so much because he represented a person like Jimmy Hoffa, but because of the tactics he used to acquit him. I too believe a man should have a fair trial without the prosecutor using unscrupulous tactics to obtain a conviction, and I think it is just as wrong for the defense counsel to use those tactics to free a man.
>
> Certainly Edward Bennett Williams had his thumb on the scales of justice when he picked Negroes for that jury and then awed them by having Joe Louis come into the courtroom and act "palsy" with Jimmy Hoffa. I believe a man should use his knowledge and skill to benefit those he loves and his fellow men, and not prostitute that knowledge and skill just for money. I didn't mean to write you a sermon, son, but I had to let you know how I felt. No one but us know the contents of this letter and disclosing it to anyone else is your choice.
> Love,
> Dad

This is the first time I have disclosed the contents of his letter to anyone. In essence, he condemned Williams for "playing a race card" in the Hoffa trial. He never said a word to me about the accusations that we had done the same thing in the O. J. trial, but neither did he offer any congratulations. I suspect he was disappointed in me. I wish he had read Williams's book before coming to the conclusion he "had his thumbs on the scale of justice." Williams offers a lengthy explanation of the Hoffa incident in his book, concluding with the following:

> The Louis story seems to grow each year and more legend and less fact gets into it. Needless to say, I'm sorry he ever came to court. But had I known he was coming to observe the trial that afternoon, I would not have asked him to stay away. I have thought about it a great deal since, and it is almost impossible to project myself back into that hectic frame of reference. But, whether it should have or not, the fact is it never crossed my mind that his presence could have any effect

on the jury. And all of the jurors later attested that his appearance at the trial was meaningless insofar as the outcome was concerned.

After the O. J. trial, I reread Edward Bennett Williams's description of what it was like to be identified as "Jimmy Hoffa's lawyer." I recalled the feeling I experienced the first time I walked through an airport and heard one passerby whisper to another, "That's one of O. J.'s lawyers." I felt proud. As the national shunning demonized O. J. Simpson despite his acquittal and turned him into a social pariah, I was well aware that some of that shunning would rub off on his lawyers. My file of hate mail testifies that some of it did. But I still feel proud. As Edward Bennett Williams put it, "For the trial lawyer, the unpopular cause is often a post of honor."

6

Thurgood Marshall*

MUCH HAS BEEN written about the unique perspectives that Justice Thurgood Marshall brought to the U.S. Supreme Court and the influence of his life experiences on conference room deliberations. One perspective is frequently overlooked in the eulogies, however, reflecting that it has all but disappeared from the U.S. Supreme Court today. It is the perspective of a criminal defense lawyer—the gut-wrenching experience of having the life or liberty of a fellow human being riding on one's tactical choices. Thurgood Marshall had been there, so he spoke with authority when the court addressed the nuances of due process and criminal law. As counsel for the NAACP Legal Defense Fund, Marshall represented dozens of criminal defendants in both trials and appeals in courtrooms across the United States. Marshall's experience as a criminal defense lawyer was most apparent in death penalty cases and strongly influenced the course of his unflagging opposition to the death penalty. That opposition was rooted in his belief that the death penalty was administered in an arbitrary and discriminatory fashion. Justice Marshall appreciated the extent to which arbitrariness and discrimination were products of the states' failures to provide adequate representation for those on trial for their lives. The cases in which he excoriated the failures and lapses of appointed counsel in death cases have a special ring of authenticity because they came from a lawyer who had himself assumed the responsibility of assigned counsel for death row inmates.

Appointed to the Supreme Court in 1967, Justice Marshall's Senate confirmation hearings were held soon after the court announced its decision in *Miranda v. Arizona*. Marshall had briefed that case as solicitor general. Senator Sam Ervin Jr. protested that the Supreme Court was "amending the Constitution" by excluding voluntary confessions. Marshall replied, "I tried a case in Oklahoma where the man 'voluntarily' confessed after he was beaten up for six days. He 'voluntarily' confessed." Senator Ervin, along with many Southern senators, voted against Thurgood Marshall's confirmation. The case Marshall referred to was *Lyons v. Oklahoma*, one of the few he lost in his thirty-two appearances to argue cases before the U.S. Supreme Court. Lyons was a young African American man accused of murdering a family of three and burning down their house to conceal the crime. He confessed after eleven days in custody. Evidence of physical brutality was disputed, but there was no dispute that the police elicited an oral confession after placing a pan of the victims' bones in Lyons's lap. He then was taken to the state prison, where the warden obtained Lyons's signature on a written confession. The prosecution did not offer the oral confession, and the U.S. Supreme Court upheld the admission of the written confession as "voluntary" by a 6–3 vote. Dissenting Justice Frank Murphy argued, "To conclude that the brutality inflicted at the time of the first confession suddenly lost all of its effect in the short space of twelve hours is to close one's eyes to the realities of human nature." Lyons certainly was not the last case in which the U.S. Supreme Court closed its eyes to the realities of human nature, but Thurgood Marshall certainly made a valiant effort in his twenty-four years on the court to keep those eyes open. Lyons, incidentally, was not a total loss for Marshall. He convinced the jury to impose a life sentence rather than the death penalty.

Not so fortunate was the nineteen-year-old African American that Thurgood Marshall represented in *Taylor v. Alabama*. Charged with the rape of a fourteen-year-old white girl, Samuel Taylor was represented by local appointed counsel who did not object to the admission of a confession made by Taylor at 3:00 a.m. to a police officer, a second admission made to the town's mayor, and a third confession made to the assistant solicitor to "get it off his chest." After Taylor was sentenced to death, the same lawyer presented an appeal to the Alabama Supreme Court, where the death sentence promptly was affirmed. Thurgood Marshall sought to challenge the voluntariness of the confession on a state writ of coram nobis and took the case to the U.S. Supreme Court when the state courts refused permission even to file the writ. Marshall lost the case by a 5–3 decision holding that states are not required to hear such claims, and his client was executed.

In another case, Marshall was trial counsel for an African American man accused of raping a white woman. The prosecution offered a life sentence in exchange for a guilty plea. Marshall conveyed the offer to his client, who exclaimed, "Plead guilty to what? Raping that woman? You gotta be kidding. I won't do it." Marshall later recounted, "That's when I knew I had an innocent man." Marshall told that story to his fellow justices, concluding, "The guy was found guilty and sentenced to death. But he never raped that woman." He paused, flicking his hand, and added, "Oh well, he was just a Negro." In a tribute to Justice Marshall after his retirement, Justice Sandra Day O'Connor reflected that stories like these "would, by and by, perhaps change the way I see the world."

The issue of the constitutionality of the death penalty came before the U.S. Supreme Court five years after Thurgood Marshall joined the court. Surprisingly, he did not base his opposition upon the arbitrariness and discrimination in its application he had seen as a lawyer. Instead, Justice Marshall's concurring opinion in *Furman v. Georgia* focused on two debatable propositions. First, he rejected retribution as a legitimate purpose of punishment under the Eighth Amendment, concluding that death was an excessive punishment because it served no legitimate governmental purpose. Second, he relied upon then-declining levels of public support for the death penalty to assert that a properly informed public would find capital punishment morally unacceptable. Four years later in *Gregg v. Georgia*, the court sustained "guided discretion" death penalty laws on the premise that the states could minimize arbitrariness and fairly and uniformly apply the punishment. Justice Marshall's dissent did not challenge this questionable premise. Instead, he returned to his *Furman* theme that retribution is not a legitimate governmental objective and that capital punishment is little more than "vestigial savagery." Justice Marshall presented his most persuasive attack on the death penalty in *Godfrey v. Georgia*. His concurring opinion drew on the court's experience since *Gregg*, decided four years earlier, and on his own experience as a defense lawyer. In his concurring opinion, Marshall suggested "why the enterprise on which the Court embarked in *Gregg v. Georgia* . . . increasingly appears to be doomed to failure." Justice Marshall found compelling evidence that the "disgraceful distorting effects of racial discrimination and poverty continue to be painfully visible in the imposition of death sentences." He pointedly reminded Justices Stewart and White that the capriciousness and attenuation

GERALD F. UELMEN

in the administration of the death penalty that led them to concur in *Furman* were still present. Concluding that eliminating arbitrariness may be a task that no criminal justice system ever can achieve, he stated, "I remain hopeful that even if the Court is unwilling to accept the view that the death penalty is so barbaric that it is in all circumstances cruel and unusual punishment forbidden by the Eighth and Fourteenth Amendments, it may eventually conclude that the effort to eliminate arbitrariness in the infliction of that ultimate sanction is so plainly doomed to failure that it—and the death penalty—must be abandoned altogether."

The manifestation of death penalty arbitrariness that drew Justice Marshall's sustained challenge during his final eight years on the court was the frequent incompetence of trial counsel appointed to defend death cases. Marshall must have been particularly disheartened to see so little improvement in the quality of appointed counsel from his personal experiences in the Supreme Court cases in the 1930s and 1940s through the 1980s. Justice Marshall assigned the responsibility for that lack of improvement to the court itself. The court's failure to articulate clear standards of competence to be applied in capital cases created no impetus for improvement. Justice Marshall sought to mobilize the bar to "find resources to establish training and assistance for local attorneys appointed to handle capital cases." While criminal defense attorneys have responded admirably to this charge, they have received little public support.

The life of Thurgood Marshall coincided with an era of incredible change in racial attitudes in America. In 1908, the year Justice Marshall was born, eighty-nine African Americans were lynched in the United States. Despite the progress of the intervening years, racism continues to pervade the administration of the death penalty in America. In 1992, the year of Thurgood Marshall's death, American states, primarily in the South, executed thirty-one convicted criminals. Nearly 40 percent of those executed were African Americans. Many were singled out for the ultimate penalty because of their poverty, lack of education, or race. As long as Justice Marshall sat on the Supreme Court, we were given persistent reminders of our failures to achieve justice in our "rush to judgment." One of the last cases presented to Justice Marshall came before the court from Ogden, Utah. The defendant, an African American, was convicted of the particularly gruesome murders of three white robbery victims. The single African American member of the jury venire was excluded, and an all-white jury was impaneled. In the midst of the trial, while the jury was eating lunch, a juror handed the bailiff a drawing on a paper napkin. The drawing depicted a man hanging from the gallows, below which the words "Hang the Niggers" were scrawled. Without conducting an evidentiary hearing to ascertain the source of the drawing, the number of jurors who had seen it, or the effect it might have had on the jurors, the judge simply instructed the jury to "ignore communications from foolish people." The federal district court denied the defendant's petition for a writ of habeas corpus, the Court of Appeals for the Tenth Circuit affirmed the denial, and the U.S. Supreme Court denied a petition for certiorari. In dissenting, Justice Marshall expressed outrage, asserting that "the Constitution, not to mention common decency," required at least an evidentiary hearing: "It is conscience shocking that all three levels of the federal judiciary are willing to send petitioner to his death without so much as investigating these serious allegations at an evidentiary hearing. Not only is this less process than due; it is no process at all."

This sense of outrage was the product of Justice Marshall's unique background. Obviously, his background as a criminal defense lawyer was only part of the personal experience Thurgood Marshall brought to his role as a judge: Justice Marshall was not only the first minority justice—he was also a nonestablishment justice. He was not an insider; his background was not one of advantage, privilege, or wealth. What is fair and just in any given situation depends on one's perspective, and Justice Marshall's perspective was different from that of his colleagues. Particularly in criminal cases, however, and especially in death penalty cases, Justice Marshall's experience as a criminal defense attorney enabled him to keep his eyes open "to the realities of human nature."

---

*   From "Justice Thurgood Marshall and the Death Penalty: A Former Criminal Defense Lawyer on the Supreme Court," *Arizona State Law Journal,* vol. 26, p. 403 (1994).

7

Ruminations on Today's Heroes*

E VERY LAWYER SHOULD have heroes to whom they look for inspiration. This is a profession in which inspiration is a necessity. At the turn of the millennium, I actually attempted to identify the "Lawyer of the Century" for the twentieth century by polling and interviewing lawyers and law students and asking them to identify their heroes. The polling produced a list of ten "contenders":

1. Clarence Darrow
2. Gerry Spence
3. Thurgood Marshall
4. Johnnie Cochran
5. F. Lee Bailey
6. William Kunstler
7. Alan Dershowitz
8. Michael Tigar
9. Edward Bennett Williams
10. Leslie Abramson

I then contacted the "contenders" who were still living and asked them whom, apart from themselves, they would consider as the greatest lawyer of the past century. Their answers were fascinating.

Leslie Abramson would pick Earl Rogers as the lawyer of the century. Rogers fell off our list of contenders, largely because so few are still familiar with his exploits today. Abramson describes Rogers as a "real" trial lawyer who fought in the courtrooms day in and day out, dazzling juries with his persuasive powers. In Rogers's day, the evidentiary battleground was the admissibility of fingerprint evidence, not DNA. Rogers fought that battle with all the wit and intelligence today's lawyers can muster. As Leslie put it, "He was the Johnnie

Cochran of his day, but smarter." She dismisses his legendary drinking problem by saying, "He could do better while drunk than most of us can do while sober." Ironically, Rogers is the lawyer Clarence Darrow himself picked to defend him when he was placed on trial in Los Angeles for jury bribery.

F. Lee Bailey's choice was Edward Bennett Williams. Soon after he passed the bar, Bailey sought an opportunity to meet Williams and asked him how he managed to pull a rabbit out of a hat so consistently. Williams told him, "If you want to pull rabbits out of hats, you better have fifty hats and fifty rabbits and get lucky." Bailey later represented a codefendant while Williams was defending Otto Kerner, a U.S. circuit judge and former governor of Illinois charged with accepting bribes. Thus, he observed Williams's legendary preparation and consummate trial skills firsthand. Bailey says that he has met or worked with every lawyer on our list of contenders with the exception of Clarence Darrow. He dismisses Darrow as a "polemicist" who shamed himself with his exploits in Los Angeles. Based upon his personal observations, Edward Bennett Williams is his "clear choice."

Johnnie Cochran did not hesitate for a second. His personal hero and choice as lawyer of the century was Thurgood Marshall. Marshall's work left a legacy that few lawyers can claim, he said. He combined great academic skills with great courtroom skills. Cochran met Marshall on the day Cochran was admitted to the bar of the U.S. Supreme Court in 1968. What impressed him most about Marshall was that "the man never forgot where he came from." Nor did Johnnie Cochran Jr.

Alan Dershowitz also picked Edward Bennett Williams as the lawyer of the century. He also placed F. Lee Bailey and Clarence Darrow near the top of his list, making it clear that only Darrow's ethical lapses would deny him the top spot. Dershowitz concluded Williams fits his "Man for All Seasons" mold because of his intelligence, tactical brilliance, and the impact of his work. When asked whom he would call if he were indicted, however, Dershowitz said his choice to represent him would be Michael Tigar.

Gerry Spence's pick for lawyer of the century was Clarence Darrow. Spence says Darrow has always been a "light" for his life. He found so great a parallel between Darrow's words and his own thoughts that he actually checked when Darrow died to see if he might have been a reincarnation of Darrow's soul! (He found he was born before Darrow's death.) While Spence does not believe in reincarnation, he certainly believes in heroes, and Darrow is his role model. He points to Darrow's passion for justice for the underdog and championing the causes of the common people as virtues for today's lawyers to emulate. He dismisses the claim that Darrow bribed jurors as unfair since Darrow can no longer defend himself and was acquitted when he could. He also suggests that even if Darrow was guilty, his conduct must be viewed in the context of the class warfare that prevailed at the time, in which the crimes of the ruling class far outweighed anything Darrow might have done.

Michael Tigar would also pick Clarence Darrow as the lawyer of the century. "No lawyer so effectively spoke to the social and historical context in which legal controversies are decided as did Darrow," he says. For him, Darrow stands in the middle of history, choosing to represent clients whose causes defined the most significant issues of the twentieth century. Tigar attributes the earliest ambitions that defined the kind of lawyer he wanted to be to reading about Darrow:

> I recall telling my father, when I was about eleven, that I was thinking of becoming a lawyer. He thought for a time, then went back to his room and came back with a copy of Irving Stone's *Clarence Darrow for the Defense*. "This," he said, "is the kind of lawyer you should be." Through high school and college I devoured books on Darrow: his autobiography, the Weinberg collection of trial excerpts, *Attorney for the Damned*, the fictionalized *Inherit the Wind*.

Tigar firmly believes that a lawyer is ultimately defined by the clients he or she chooses to represent. Even the most unpopular client can present an opportunity to advance the cause of justice. In defending Terry Nichols, Tigar reread many of Darrow's great arguments to find inspiration. With regard to the charge of jury bribing, Tigar reflects that many great lawyers were accused of unduly influencing juries, but Darrow is the only one "with a certificate saying he is not guilty." "If we believe in our system of justice," he concludes, "we have to assume Darrow was innocent."

From the contenders' perspectives, Edward Bennett Williams may have an equal claim with that of Clarence Darrow. Yet none of our contenders was closer to Edward Bennett Williams than Michael Tigar, having worked with Williams's law firm. His selection of Darrow is based upon the causes Darrow served and the issues he litigated.

Williams and Darrow represent two very different images of the American lawyer. Williams was ultimately the Washington insider, who carefully picked clients who would enhance that image. Darrow, however, had no qualms about being perceived as a radical who was ready to challenge conventional wisdom; and he picked clients whose causes challenged the prevailing hypocrisy. Williams had great impact upon the law, especially in areas of privacy rights and wiretapping. But Darrow's causes spoke to a broader audience. He did indeed "plead for the future."

---

* From "Who Is the Lawyer of the Century?" *Loyola of Los Angeles Law Review,* vol. 33, p. 613 (2000).

Edwards Brothers Malloy
Oxnard, CA USA
April 5, 2016